THE ART OF SPYRO

REIGNITED TRILOGY

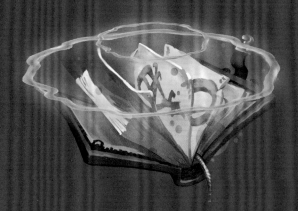

WRITTEN BY

MICKY NEILSON

FOREWORD BY

JOSH NADELBERG

TITAN BOOKS

TABLE OF CONTENTS

8 | FOREWORD

10 | INTRODUCTION

14 | Spyro

18 | Heroes & Villains

44 | Dragons

94 | Friends & Enemies

152 | The World of Spyro

287 | ACKNOWLEDGMENTS

288 | COLOPHON

FOREWORD

BY JOSH NADELBERG

I was in the ninth grade when home consoles moved from 8 to 16 bit, and my mind was blown! The richness of the worlds I was exploring, the colors, the detail . . . Those games sucked me in and awed me with their unbelievable 16-bit graphics! How could video games possibly look this rich and beautiful?

I was in college when the next generation of consoles came around with 64-bit graphics, and again . . . Mind Blown! How was I ever going to go to class when I could run around in these amazing 3D worlds? My GPA was surely impacted, but I was hooked.

It wasn't too long after that when a little Purple Dragon was born into the world and millions of people were instantly sucked into the Dragon Realms, cursing those pesky egg thieves and searching for every epic crystal dragon to rescue. To all of us in 1998, the world of *Spyro the Dragon™* was the most magical and beautiful place to explore. It captivated fans, delighted and inspired a generation of gamers, and etched itself in our memories.

Memories... When I learned that the next project for Toys for Bob would be a remastering of the classic *Spyro™ the Dragon* trilogy developed by Insomniac Games, it was the memory of playing those early 3D games from 20 years ago that came rushing back. We get to remake Gnasty Gnorc, and Ripto? Those Creepy Spiders in High Caves? All those awesome dragons??? I couldn't wait to get started.

Now, the tricky thing with memories is that they sometimes come with a big old pair of what we call rose-tinted glasses. Such was the case with my memory of Spyro™, where the beauty and splendor of the originals were as pure as they were on the day I first experienced them, unsullied by twenty years of technological advances and three entire console generations. As we began to wrap our heads around the project, we felt like it was our responsibility to deliver fans the game they remembered, to give them the experience of playing it all again for the first time, which meant making it look as rich and immersive as any other game they could choose to play today. It was with that intention that we set to work.

One thing that we hadn't yet quite wrapped our heads around was the scope and ambition of the project that we were about to embark on. I mean, these were twenty-year-old games. How much content could there possibly be? Well, it turns out that one of the reasons we all loved Spyro so much back in the day was because the games were huge! Each had dozens of beautiful levels full of hidden nooks and crannies with themes that ranged from surreal floating castles in the clouds to giant treetop villages. They were chock-full of literally hundreds of unique and incredibly off-the-wall characters with bespoke animations and behaviors. There were three games, and we set out to recreate them all from scratch.

Making the *Spyro™ Reignited Trilogy* was a leap of faith—full of exhilaration, hope, wonder, fear, and doubt. We had the most delightful source material to work from that anyone could possibly imagine, an amazingly talented team, and an organization who believed in us and supported us every step of the way. But more than anything, we knew that we were working on something that was going to mean so much to people whose memories of Spyro were formative and profound.

This book is just a tiny slice of the art of the Spyro™ Reignited Trilogy. It is the work of wild and wonderful imaginations and incredibly talented and passionate artists and illustrators who gladly put on those rose-tinted glasses and tried to capture what they saw to bring the world of Spyro back to life.

INTRODUCTION

"There was just so much to do! Planning it all, finding the right people, and just believing that we could accomplish it and do all the work. It was overwhelming. But it was also a challenge that everybody rose to, and that was awesome. I think we found folks that were passionate about it and were having fun with it and put a lot of energy and effort and passion and love into making it." —JOSH NADELBERG

Crash course

For Toys For Bob studios, the drive to reignite Spyro was given a boost by a different anthropomorphic critter altogether. According to Studio Head Paul Yan:

"The success of the Crash Bandicoot™ N. Sane Trilogy took everyone by surprise - it was crystal clear that fans really wanted to take a nostalgic trip to their earliest console gaming memories. It was a no-brainer that we should apply the same care and authenticity to the one and only Spyro."

The announcement of the *Spyro Reignited Trilogy* was met with tears—the good kind—from fans. Players fondly remembered hours spent in front of their consoles and anxiously anticipated a remaster of their beloved game.

Toys For Bob tackled the initial development of the *Spyro Reignited Trilogy* on three different fronts: First, they dusted off and booted up a plethora of old consoles to play the classic game on. Second, they put the Quality Assurance team to work cataloguing everything in the old trilogy, from the number of enemies per level to the specific placement of each and every gem. And third, they set out to analyze as much data from the original metrics as possible. This last proved the most challenging, but Toys For Bob rose to

the task through a nifty little invention called the Spyroscope (which we'll learn more about in the World of Spyro intro).

As all these wheels were set into motion, Toys For Bob made sure not to lose sight of the main goal, described here by Paul:

"Early on, we all were in agreement that success for us with a remaster would mean that someone who was a fan of the original games could pick up the game and their muscle memory would just kick in, and they would be familiar with the controls without having to be onboarded. All their nostalgia should help them into that experience, so that became a pillar for us, which was 'design is in parity with the spirit of the original game.' We were going for authenticity as much as possible."

Hey, this is an art book. Let's talk about art!

Great idea! Remastering the art from the original Spyro games was a daunting task but one eagerly embraced by art director Josh Nadelberg.

For Josh, who had gotten used to developing intellectual properties from scratch, stepping into an already-established world was a nice change of pace. Adapting a beloved classic, however, also came with its own set of challenges.

Spyro was created back in 1998, along with all the technological limitations of that time. In fact, there are more polygons in Spyro's eyes in the *Spyro Reignited Trilogy* than there were in his entire original character model! Although this meant the artists would have ample freedom to pursue their own interpretations, it also meant there was a danger of the art going too far astray. Remember Paul talking about parity of design with the spirit of the original game? Well, that held true just as much for the art as it did for the game design. Thus began a tightrope walk for the project that would continue throughout the development of the Spyro Reignited Trilogy, described by Josh as

"striking a balance between being very reverential and honoring the spirit of the original games while still allowing and fostering a sense of almost limitless creativity with the artists who were working on it."

It takes a village, people

Once those industrious QA folks had catalogued their hearts out, the sheer volume of art that would be needed for the *Spyro Reignited Trilogy* became very clear. It was a project that was going to demand a *lot* of art from a lot of different artists. According to Josh,

"The neat thing about the way we set up the art team was that we don't have a huge art team here at Toys For Bob, so there were all these amazing artists from all around the world that got together."

Once the fellowship was gathered, it was time to get everyone on the same artistic page. And that's where the art bible came in.

The art bible was a helpful little guide put together by Josh to serve as a kind of creative roadmap, outlining things like shape language and how detailed the art should be in order for the game to have a consistent look. The guidance provided in the bible applied not just to the overall style but gave specifics intended for characters and environments as well. (And because of that, you'll see it referenced at various points throughout this book!)

Also in the early stages of development, a great deal of time and effort went into getting the look of Spyro just right. Toys For Bob had familiarity with the purple dragon already, having included him in their *Skylanders®* series. Skylanders, however, was a much different game, with a much different style. This made for a tricky process in perfecting Spyro for the *Reignited Trilogy*.

While the purple dragon went through multiple iterations, the members of the art team not working on that task were able to cut loose on Spyro's sometimes bizarre but always interesting stable of supporting characters. As Josh explained,

"It was very clear what we needed to make, so it was like, 'Who's gonna have a great time designing the dudes in the second game who are capybaras on race cars and motorboats? Ryan [Jones], you're gonna have a blast making capybaras on motorboats.'"

And, of course, let's not forget environments. Spyro and that crazy cast of characters needed equally fun and engaging levels to run around in!

Objects in the rearview mirror

In November of 2018, the finished game was unleashed on fans all over the world.

So, was it all worth it? Did Toys For Bob achieve the goal of parity with the spirit of the original game? Most importantly, what did gamers think? Josh had this to say:

"The most proud moment was reading people's reactions where they said, 'You know what? This is exactly how it felt to me when I played the original game.' We tried our best to honor the fact that people have really important, formative memories of this game, and there were some really touching stories in videos that people posted around the game and

memories they had with it, how important it was for them, and to know that we made them proud and brought something back around for them—that was really special."

And, one thing all of the artists interviewed for this book agreed on: working on *Spyro Reignited Trilogy* was a ton of fun.

Now, you'll get a peek behind the curtain to see just how Toys For Bob and some of the world's most renowned artists collaborated to develop one of the most anticipated games.

We'll explore all the things that made Spyro Reignited Trilogy great, beginning with the little purple fella himself and then diving deeper into the dragons, the heroes and bosses, the friends and enemies, and the game's stunning environments.

Looks like you've got lots to do! So go ahead, turn the page . . .

And let the adventure begin!

ART STYLE PHILOSOPHY

1. Stay true to the spirit of the original: Capture the magic of what it was like to play Spyro for the first time.

2. What might other developers do with Spyro today? What can we glean from other platformer games and art styles?

3. Create a believable fantasy/fairy-tale world by focusing on storytelling in all aspects of the visual design, and take every opportunity to inject fun into the world.

4. Don't feel constrained by a formula. There is room for breadth within the style. The formula will squash delightful variety and discourage discovery.

5. Push playfulness and personality to the limits!

6. Extreme shape play will be the glue that binds it all together and defines the style.

7. There's a huge community of adult gamers who played Spyro as a kid. Let's make sure to make the experience fresh and appealing to them, while still staying true to the youthful appeal of Spyro.

Spyro

ALL ABOUT OUR MAIN DRAGON

⟲ *"We knew we had to get Spyro just right! There have been a bunch of interpretations of the character over the years, and we wanted to make him timeless. We wanted people to see our new Spyro and think, 'That's just like I remember him' and 'Wow, he looks so cool.'"*

—JOSH NADELBERG

Artistic Expression

One of the primary elements Art Director Josh Nadelberg focused on from the beginning with Spyro was his relatability. Toys For Bob viewed Spyro as "the hero we all see in ourselves." To that end, they wanted to make him "super cute, super charming, but to have that feel in his eye that he could do this, he could save the world."

In the very beginning, a study of facial expressions was completed to determine the range of emotions, expressions, and acting that the team might expect to get from Spyro. The sketches were handed to animators to make a first-pass 3D model, and the result was extremely well received. Per Josh,

"We were like, 'Oh my God, they've managed to create a character here, not a 3D model. We're making video games, but I want to see movies about this guy. I want to see these characters in TV shows. I really believe in the fear in his eyes. I believe in the surprise. I believe in all of these emotions that they were pulling out of the model."

A special kickoff

With the team ready to go into production, Toys For Bob wanted to meet with Insomniac Games, the team that created Spyro. Activision had worked with a company called First 4 Figures to create a Spyro statue based on the original box art, and Paul Yan brought one to the meeting and assembled it.

Paul recalls the rest of the meeting:

"We set it aside as we had a long conversation, showed him [Insomniac CEO Ted Price] our concept art, and toward the end, I turned to him and said, 'There's gonna be a million decisions that we're gonna be making to try and make this as authentic as possible. If there's one thing that we can get right, what do we need to pour all of our attention into?' He said 'make sure you pay attention to the details, especially with Spyro himself.' At that moment, he turned to the statue and said, 'take this statue for instance.' He told us how the game version of Spyro and what ended up being the model that showed up on the box art were completely different processes, so the representation that ended up being on the box art isn't actually true to what the game character was like. The proportions were different, like the crest of the chest, the length of the legs, the nail length, the brow shape was very different—but he was quick to say, 'Look at all these things, pay special attention to those' and that gave us a real appreciation for the details and how we refined our version of the character."

The eyes have it

Josh called on concept artist and illustrator Nicholas Kole to help address some of the feedback and refine the design. The assignment was a dream for Nicholas, who spent his youth tracing the dragon from magazine illustrations.

One of the early changes that was made involved Spyro's chest, which was changed from ribbed and scaly to having tough breastplating. The intent was to give him the feel of a kid puffing out his chest to look and feel stronger.

After a fair bit of tweaking, TFB took their revised tough-guy version of Spyro back to Insomniac for feedback. With the changes they had made, Josh and the rest of the team were anxious about Insomniac's impression.

"I remember Ted Price looked at the updated Spyro and he was like, 'It's all in the eyes.' And I was like, 'Okay, tell me, what is it about the eyes?' The illustrations had Spyro just staring really intently, and there was white all around his eyes, and he's like, 'We should not see so much of the whites of his eyes.' In the original game, one thing that really defined Spyro was that his eye should always be intersecting with the purple around his eye on the bottom, or if he's looking to the side—it should never be floating. He was totally right, and we tried to adjust based on that feedback."

Economy of scale

Nicholas continued refining, fixing Spyro's eyes and strengthening his shapes, colors, and silhouette. Another main focus during the dragon's early development phase was his scales.

The idea was to harken back to Spyro's roots while also giving him Toys For Bob's unique visual spin. Having started with a "busy" scale texture, the team switched gears and began to simplify, with the aim of achieving a cleaner, more playful, and cartoony representation. To do this, they focused on soft gradients and bits of detail—patches of dark scale shapes on Spyro's shoulders or in subtle areas around his face. The purpose of detail in Spyro became more clearly defined: to help express character and enhance design. Josh felt that this choice had a ripple effect and helped set the stylistic tone for the entire game.

Another element of Spyro's design that Nicholas felt particularly passionate about was Spyro's paws. Nicholas drew inspiration from the Spyro community and fans, as well as the idea of Spyro being a kind of "dragon pup," with paws that were just a little too big that he would eventually grow into.

When they felt they had it, they sent an update to Insomniac, and it was met with enthusiasm and excitement. This new Spyro was ready to burn!

Born to glide

If the fan response was any indication (and it was), the attention to detail paid off. The reviews were overwhelmingly positive, with many players feeling as if they had put on their nostalgia goggles and time-traveled back to 1998.

For Toys For Bob, their proudest moments came from knowing that they had done what they set out to do: stay faithful to the spirit of the original and put their own stylistic stamp on a character that was and still is, in the words of Nicholas Kole, "a timeless mascot."

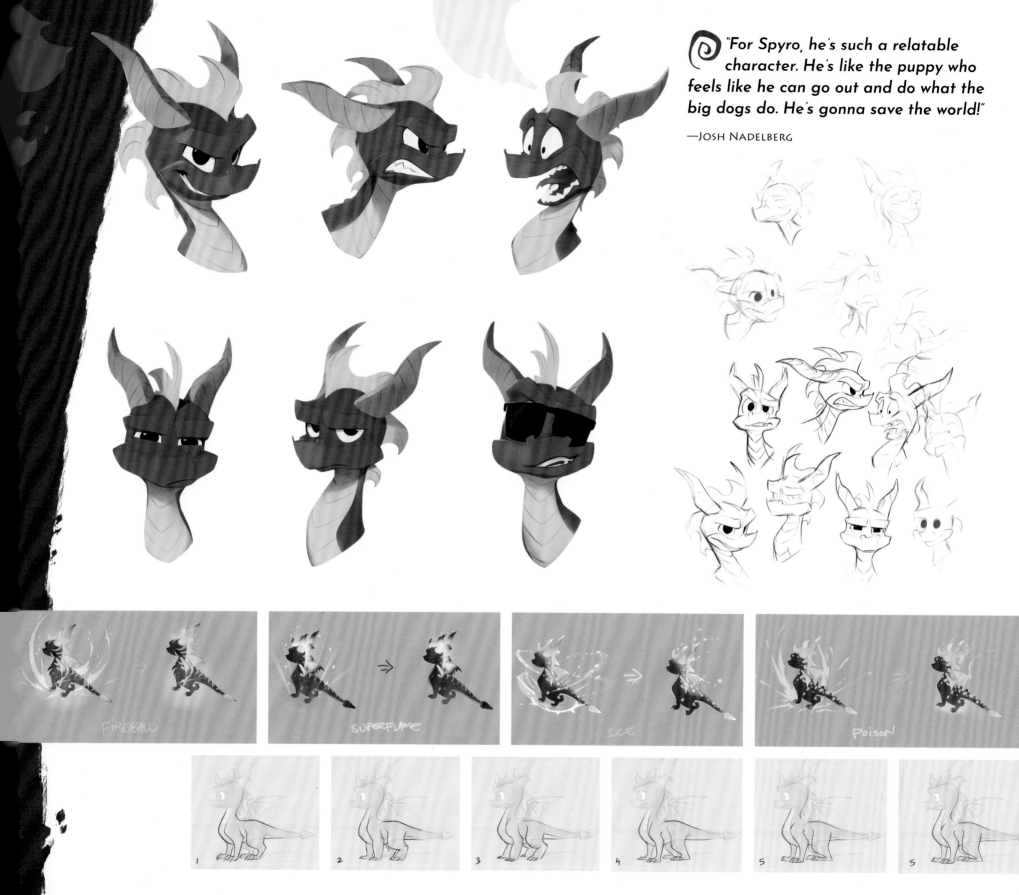

FIREBALL

SUPERFLAME

ICE

POISON

1   2   3   4   5   5

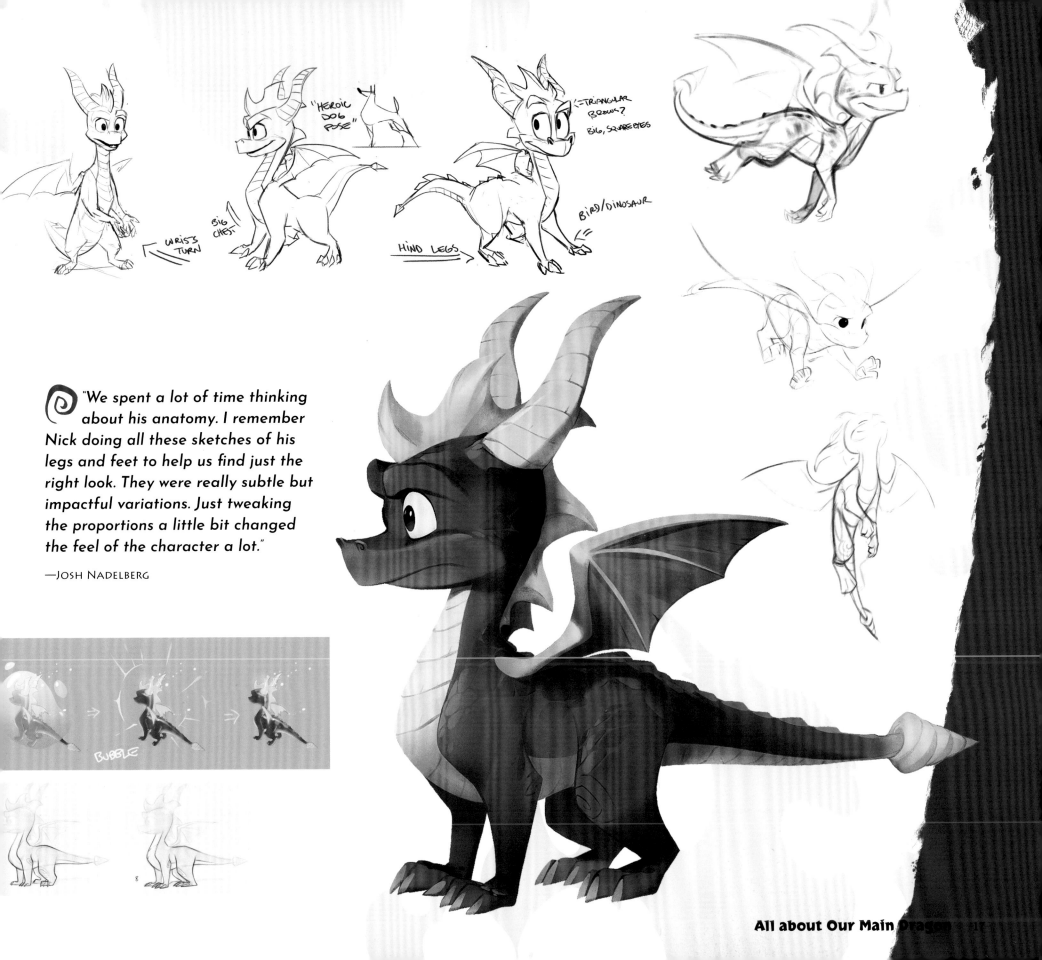

"HEROIC DOG POSE"

WRIST TURN

BIG CHEST

TRIANGULAR BROWS?

BIG, SQUARE EYES

HIND LEGS

BIRD/DINOSAUR

"We spent a lot of time thinking about his anatomy. I remember Nick doing all these sketches of his legs and feet to help us find just the right look. They were really subtle but impactful variations. Just tweaking the proportions a little bit changed the feel of the character a lot."

—JOSH NADELBERG

BUBBLE

Heroes & Villains

○ *"I'm a big believer in immersion early on in a project. It's really important for me to get as much information as possible and gather as much reference and tidbits of lore and details of the character and the fandom and understanding who the other people are who love this and how can I be inspired by that energy."*

—NICHOLAS KOLE

The good, the bad, and the Gnasty

A talking cheetah, a mole in a lab coat, a faun in a corset, a rabbit in a cape, a safari kangaroo, and a military penguin . . . No, this isn't the setup to some elaborate joke, it's just part of the hero lineup from the first three Spyro games. The original trilogy reflected the overall aesthetic and sensibilities of '90s games—in the words of artist Devon Cady-Lee, who worked on several characters for the *Reignited Trilogy*:

"A lot of it was more of a wacky, [loony], gross humor—the '90s were very fun and out there and extreme."

In the first game, *Spyro the Dragon*, our purple protagonist was pretty much a solo hero act, running around saving adult dragons with the aid of his companion, the dragonfly Sparx. There was, however, no shortage of bosses for Spyro to fight, with a total of six throughout the game, including the main villain, Gnasty Gnorc. In the follow-up, *Spyro™ 2: Ripto's Rage*, the adult dragons from the first game were absent. New major characters—Elora the Faun, Hunter the Cheetah, and the Professor—were introduced, along with four new bosses and the main baddie, Ripto. The third game saw Hunter make a comeback and debuted four new heroes—a kangaroo, penguin, yeti, and monkey—along with a bevy of bruiser bosses commanded by the evil Sorceress.

A cut above

Most of the character interaction in the first three games was conveyed through cut scenes. When Toys For Bob took on *Spyro Reignited Trilogy*, they decided to leave the stories of all three games intact, although they did set about making changes to the cut scenes—mainly altering camera angles and character placement, along with adjustments that clarified gags or story beats that were ambiguous in the original. The overall goal in modifying the cut scenes was, in the words of Toys For Bob studio head Paul Yan, to "highlight and elevate" the narrative and its intentions.

Another step in the process of highlighting and elevating those intentions came in the form of updating all of the main characters with new and improved versions, a process that originated in the concept stage, with illustrators under the leadership of art director Josh Nadelberg.

Sound advice

One of the early approaches illustrators took was to capture the main characters' personalities through the vocal performances of classic Spyro. The voice work helped guide artists in remaining faithful to the tone of the original while modifying everything from the characters' overall general design to their body language. Guided by the art bible we mentioned way back in the main intro, concept creators worked hard to ensure they captured the spirit of the original games' crazy, cartoony, and playful tone. Once artists had a good handle on the style, the process of character design came much more easily.

Hits and misses

The art team was aware from the outset that they were dealing with time-tested and fondly remembered characters. As designs rolled out and were released to the public, fan responses were immediate and provided an instant gauge—good and bad—of how the new characters were being received. The decision to put legs on Spyro's dragonfly companion, Sparx, for instance, went over like a Gnorc party-crasher at a *Year of the Dragon* bash.

Other changes met with instant excitement and were not only accepted but embraced by the community. One such case was Elora, a faun hero from the second game. Her model became one of the largest departures from the source character; artist Nicholas Kole changed her hair, added deerlike features to her face, and gave her a shorter tail and cloven hooves. Her costume went from a green corset to a leaf dress. As opposed to the remastered Sparx, the adjustments to Elora met with praise. According to Nicholas,

"We got a lot of great fan art from the community. People really embraced the design. It was a really cool success, but it was a controversial one because we moved away and I led a move away from the source material on that one because it felt like some of these moments from 1999 survived the test of time and others not so much."

"Every good battle needs a good adversary."

In the process of designing the bosses, shape language was a key ingredient. Artists used shape repetition to blend elements of the characters together and to create a more cohesive design. One specific example was the case of Ripto, the main villain in *Spyro 2: Ripto's Rage*. Nicholas Kole utilized curling shapes that echoed Ripto's horn throughout the costume, including his collar and coattails. Also, elements of the outfit were exaggerated in size to accentuate the villain's miniature stature—something that was mirrored in the villain's staff, with the large gem atop the short shaft mimicking the boss's oversized cranium atop his small body.

For the design of Gnasty Gnorc, the main villain of game one, artist Nicola Saviori highlighted and exaggerated the boss's weapon and pushed and distorted various shapes, such as the Gnorc's mouth and the spikes on his armor. While Gnasty Gnorc's teeth were slightly exaggerated, Nicola was careful to avoid making them overly sharp or grotesque, something that would have altered the character's tone and placed him outside the established world of Spyro.

Sketches were also made specifically showing the villains in action, performing an attack or sometimes portraying the way they were defeated, a tactic that allowed artists to further home in on their design. In addition to illustrating what it was the villains were doing, the art team gave considerable thought to the environment they would perform those actions in, especially when choosing a color palette. Artists used complementary colors, contrasts, and shades to make the characters pop off the background. And, they were careful to use variations in hue and saturation to stay away from harsh shadows and stark blacks that would lend the game a darker overall tone.

Fan-tastic

Working on Spyro Reignited Trilogy gave artists a new appreciation for what early game developers were able to do with limited disk space. The differences between classic Spyro characters and the remastered versions were striking. For many artists, getting to see their concepts realized in the game's finished 3D models was a significant reward for their many hours of hard work. Perhaps the greatest reward, however, was the fan mail, fan art, tattoos, tear-filled social media videos, and stories of families bonding over hours of gameplay—all fitting tributes to the studio and the art team that enhanced and elevated Spyro's characters for a whole new generation . . . and for many generations to come.

HEROES

"The original design in the old games had this ribb... ...ly... ...at went a... ...belly... ...didn't have... ...top... ...that... ...that was something w... ...ra... ...i... ...ly... ...ove... ...bit the most of the des... ...K... ...you're... ...so... ...it... ...the s... ...sc... ...a... ...e... ...re... ...bout..."

Sparx

"You're looking through the old models for visual cues, but you're also looking at everything else you can to get hints at what might be a really good and faithful way to move it forward."

—Nicholas Kole

Hunter

Elora

🌀 *"People really embraced the design. That was a really cool success, but it was a controversial one because we moved away from the original design on that one."*

—NICHOLAS KOLE

Bianca

 *"With Elora, Bianca, and Hunter, I knew they were big fan favorites from back in the day, so I really wanted to make sure that I watched videos of the old games to hear vocal performances, and I tried to really design their faces and personalities and even their body language in the concepts that communicate that attitude."*

—Nicholas Kole

 *"When we started looking at Sheila, we noticed that she was a bit simple compared to some of the other characters. She had no accessories or details. She's just a kangaroo. We asked the concept artists to take some liberties to enhance her personality."*

—Josh Nadelberg

Sheila

The Professor

"When I asked Nick to close his eyes and give him that squinty mole expression, that's when we found the Professor. I remember the animators wondering if he should ever open his eyes at all!"

—JOSH NADELBERG

Agent 9

"The first concept that we did of Agent 9 leaned in hard on the crazy side of his personality. It was a wee bit too freaky, with scars on his cheeks and this broken-looking tail, so we backed off a bit in the final version."

—Josh Nadelberg

Sgt. Byrd

"The biggest challenge was trying to be true to some of the characters, especially if they were fan favorites. Luckily, there are resources devoted to a lot of the lore and the backstory."

—Ryan Jones

Bentley

VILLAINS

Gnasty Gnorc

"For Gnasty Gnorc, we were imagining him as this insecure tough guy who's deeply wounded when the dragons call him ugly. We leaned into that and thought that he was like this weight lifter at the gym who spends hours on his upper body but never works out his legs. We kept pushing those proportions till it was perfectly over the top."

—Tom NAPIERTO

"The creation of Gnasty Gnorc was particularly satisfying because it was precisely the type of character I prefer, rancorous and vindictive but also with funny and goofy nuances that don't make it a bidimensional villain but with different facets."

—Nicola SAVIORI

OLD LOOK

NEW LOOK

A.

B.

C.

D.

Toasty

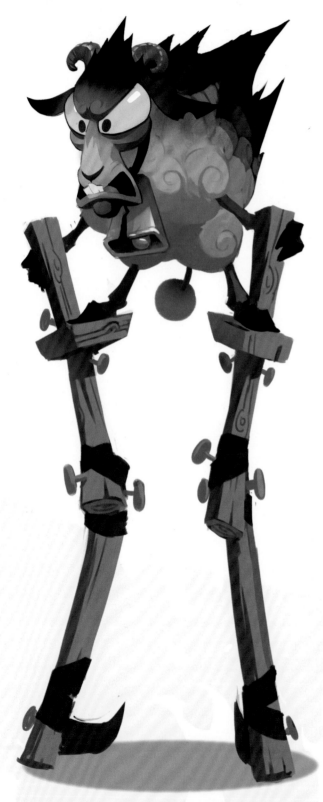

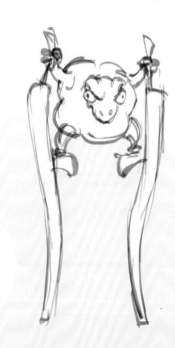

"Seeing Toasty finally put together and having him move around and doing all the gags he did in the first game—that was a very proud moment."

—Devon Cady-Lee

"Toasty was the first boss that we reimagined and implemented. I felt like we took quite a risk with his design. We leaned into a darker, quirkier, edgier take on the character while still trying to retain the cartoony absurdity of the character. It was very well received and gave us a ton of confidence as we moved forward."

—JOSH NADELBERG

"I was looking at other '90s products and things from that time period. I was trying to see what strung them together, and a lot of it was wacky, gross humor. The '90s were very fun and out there and extreme."

—DEVON CADY-LEE

TOASTY

STRAW

SHEEP BELL ?!

Doctor Shemp

"For Spyro, I tried to produce several sketches that showed the characters in some actions performed in the game, such as a special attack, a particular movement, or the way they were defeated. The combination of these drawings helps to enrich the character and better define his personality within the game."

—Nicola Saviori

Blowhard

"Blowhard was such a trip! He's a floating beard with a hat and arms. I knew that Oleg [Yurkov] would be the perfect artist to work on his redesign. His process involves these wonderfully expressive animatic movement explorations, and those were really helpful in capturing the character."

—Josh Nadelberg

Ripto

"Within the context of the story, Ripto's a runt and has a bit of a Napoleon complex, and so trying to use the shape language and really exaggerate—with his collar and the jewel hanging off his neck—his dimunitive size made that a more fun and playful storytelling moment."

—NICHOLAS KOLE

"I really wanted him to feel like he was swimming in his collar. I loved the spiraling horn motif and wanted to create this devil horn shape with the collar, and I wanted to echo that in the shoes that curl up and even the tail of his coat, and they all create these curling horn shapes that reinforce that shape language."

—NICHOLAS KOLE

Metalhead

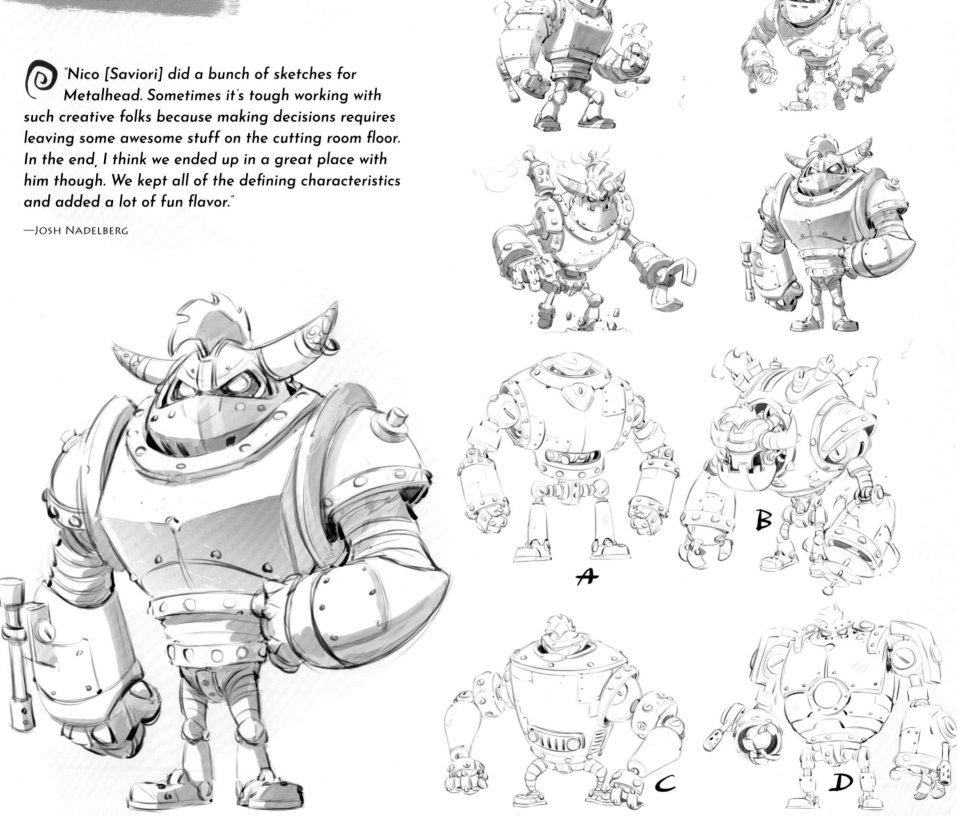

"Nico [Saviori] did a bunch of sketches for Metalhead. Sometimes it's tough working with such creative folks because making decisions requires leaving some awesome stuff on the cutting room floor. In the end, I think we ended up in a great place with him though. We kept all of the defining characteristics and added a lot of fun flavor."

—Josh Nadelberg

A

B

C

D

Jacques

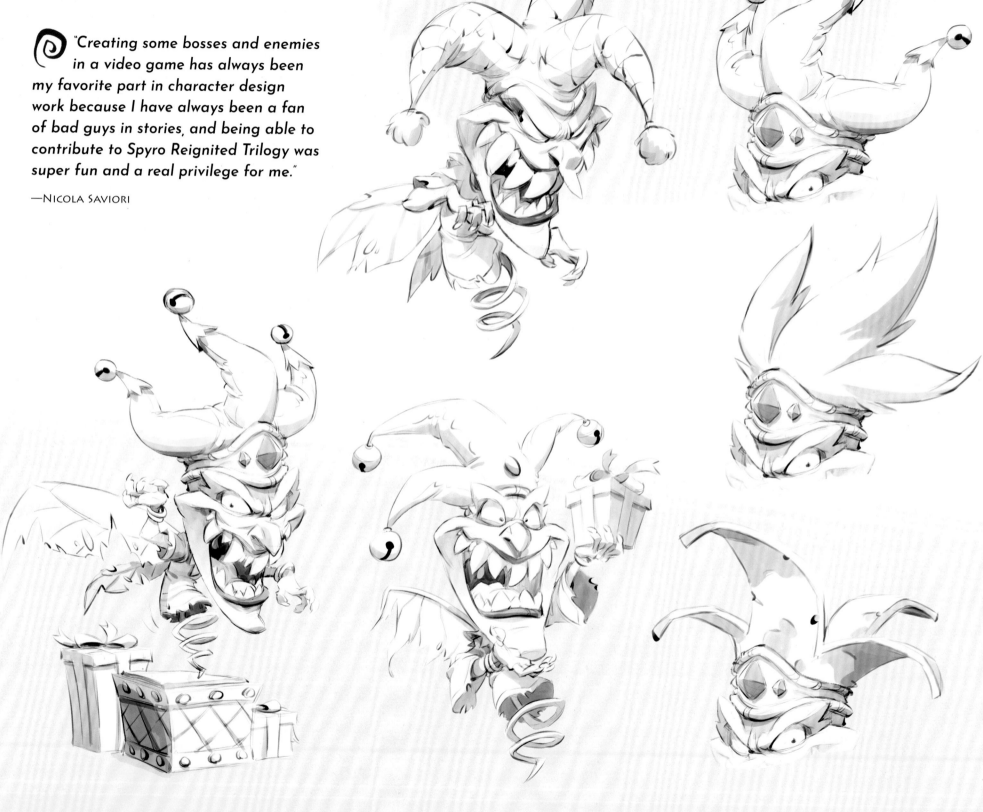

 "Creating some bosses and enemies in a video game has always been my favorite part in character design work because I have always been a fan of bad guys in stories, and being able to contribute to Spyro Reignited Trilogy was super fun and a real privilege for me."

—Nicola Saviori

Gulp

Crush

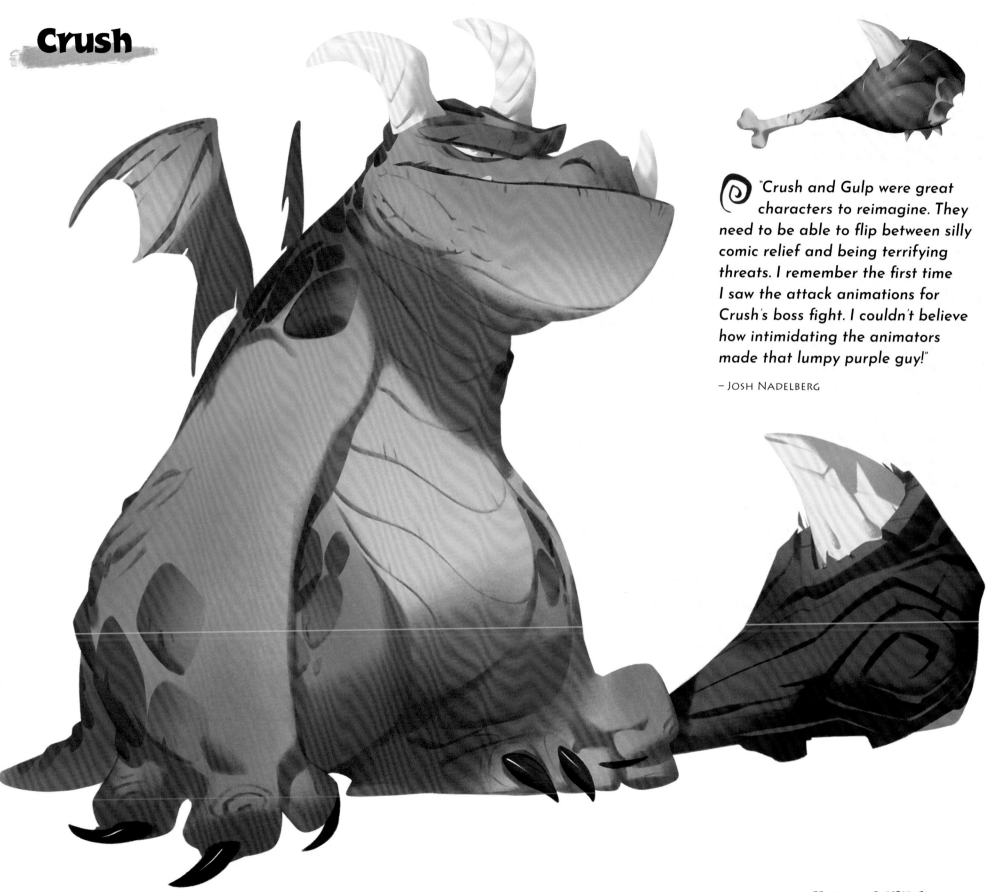

"Crush and Gulp were great characters to reimagine. They need to be able to flip between silly comic relief and being terrifying threats. I remember the first time I saw the attack animations for Crush's boss fight. I couldn't believe how intimidating the animators made that lumpy purple guy!"

– JOSH NADELBERG

Buzz

Scorch

Sorceress

"Like we learned with Spyro, so much of the character is in the eyes. The Sorceress concept had this great expression that we really wanted to replicate just right in 3D. I spent a lot of time with the 3D artist to get the size of her pupils, the thickness of the lashes, the colors— everything—just right."

—JOSH NADELBERG

Dragons

⊙ *"The work on dragons, unlike the other creatures and enemies in the game where we were more free, was more controlled and binding. Dragons belong to different categories, and these must be visible and easily identifiable in the character's design."*

—Nicola Saviori

Math, what about it?

In classic Spyro, each adult dragon had its own name, voice, and color. Beyond that, however, there was very little variation from one to the next because all dragons were built from just a few different models with a limited polygon budget.

For Spyro Reignited Trilogy, this provided an opportunity for Toys For Bob to not just uprez the models but to provide each and every dragon with its own identity. Art director Josh Nadelberg confided half-jokingly, or maybe half-seriously,

"We were stupidly ambitious and decided to make each one of them unique."

This was an exciting goal but one that posed an immediate problem. Remember those hard-charging, tirelessly cataloguing QA folks from the main intro? Well, the fruits of their labors made it immediately apparent that the greatest challenge TFB would face in creating new and different dragons would be sheer volume. There were almost ninety dragons in the first game. Surely that daunting number would be enough to make Toys For Bob rethink their strategy, right?
Wrong!

TFB: Not dragon their feet

Josh led the charge, working with both internal and external artists on concepts intended to nail down the overall dragons' look and feel. The early results had Josh excited:

"There were a couple pages of expressions and different dragon designs that Devon

[Cady-Lee] had done that, all of a sudden, it was like, 'Oh yes, that is the feel that I want these dragons to have.' It was this charming, really approachable, really wise, really silly, but grand flavor that he got in those faces. I remember seeing that page and being like, 'Yes!"

Giving each dragon a memorable personality was a huge goal from the beginning. As a result, a lot of early work centered around dragon faces, a process that led to all sorts of interesting experiments and whimsical explorations, including concepts inspired by styles ranging from rock star to wholesome painter.

Weaving the dream

There were five main factions or schools of dragons in the original Spyro that aligned with five out of the six main levels in the game: Artisans, Peace Keepers, Magic Crafters, Beast Makers, and Dream Weavers. According to studio head Paul Yan,

"We took that as a starting point and said, 'How do we take that idea and continue with that?' So thinking about those themes, we built out individually those different dragons and said, 'Okay this is an artisan dragon. What does an Artisan dragon look like? Well, it's a dragon that specializes in arts and crafts, so this one's going to be a musician, this one's going to be a painter . . .' So that gave us the starting point to push forward."

A lot of time and consideration went into differentiating the dragons visually, according to the factions they belonged to. This allowed the artists to spread their wings (pun fully intended) as they explored various ideas and interpretations, all while remaining faithful to the spirit of the classic Spyro. From Paul:

"There were a lot of artists from all around the world contributing to this, and a good number of them grew up with Spyro, and they were basically the perfect demographic for it. So we were able to lean on their nostalgia and their sensibilities for what was appropriate, what was skewing too far into reinterpreting what the world was like and, what was more in line with canon, and what was implied in the original games. With art direction, you have stylistic guardrails but the artists had a lot of latitude to push the ideas as far as they could, and we encouraged that as much as possible."

As the process evolved, it wasn't uncommon for a concept that started off as one character to be transferred over to another. Josh recalls,

"Sometimes you'd see something that would work great here and shift it over there. There was a little bit of that, especially with the dragons because there were so many of them, and sometimes they would come up with some personality or some character in one of the dragons, and you're like, 'Oh, that would be amazing if we used it for the one who had this silly voice line.'"

Getting into shape

Each dragon Spyro rescued in the game only had a few lines of dialogue, usually helpful hints for gameplay. After dispensing their sage advice, the dragons would disappear, and most would not be seen again. This limited voice-over and screen time meant that each dragon's backstory had to be conveyed mostly through the art, something that was done not only through props and costume but also through shape language and repeating shape elements.

Where classic Spyro had only a couple body types for the dragons, TFB created body types for each faction and built from there. One example of this was the Peace Keepers, mighty dragon protectors who were drawn as muscular and top-heavy, a contrast to the thin, more laid-back Dream Weavers. The trick for artists was to create as much variation within the body types as possible by manipulating those base proportions.

Repeating shape elements were used especially in the wings and horns of the individual dragons, but also more subtly in the facial structure, such as the sharpness of cheekbones or jaws.

Sometimes artists drew inspiration for shape language from the area the dragon would be found in. For dragons that were found in a jungle setting, for instance, jungle animal anatomy was used in the character's concept design and incorporated into the dragon's anatomy.

In the end, the concept artists' work was brought to life through 3D modeling, texturing, and voice-over work. The real winners, however, were the gamers. Because with every dragon Spyro rescued, players were rewarded with a carefully crafted, unique, and unforgettable character.

"When they already had so many dragons, it was like puzzle-solving, like a form of color sudoku, you're just trying to work in 'what colors haven't we used' and 'this one's going to stand out from the other' but without it turning into a kaleidoscopic mess."

—ROB DUENAS

ARTISANS

🌀 "Once we decided to lean into giving the dragons all of this additional character and personality, it opened up this whole new problem set of what exactly each dragon's thing would be and why. We tried to take cues from their dialogue and location in the level whenever possible, but sometimes, we just had fun with it. The very first round of ideation on the dragons was much simpler and faithful to the spirit of the original designs."

—Josh Nadelberg

Delbin

"Nick always added such great details. Delbin introduces you to Sparx, so having him be this big hunky painter with a portrait of Sparx on his easel was aces."

—JOSH NADELBERG

Gavin

"I remember brain-storming with Nick about what type of artisan Gavin should be. We had done sculptors, painters, potters . . . Nick suggested he could be an artisan coffee roaster! We laughed about it, and then he drew Gavin. It was great fun working together."

—Josh Nadelberg

"He [Gildas] has a paintbrush, but his tail is also turned into a paintbrush. There's this alchemist dragon I did who uses his wings as a chalkboard. So it would be a repurposing of their anatomy to associate it strongly with their faction."

—DEVON CADY-LEE

Gildas

Lindar

Tomas

Argus

Oswin

Astor

"*An early design of Nestor became Oswin, as he fit perfectly in the library, and the original Revilo found a home in the Dream Weavers as Oswin. Did you get all that? Here they are in their original concept colors.*"

—Josh Nadelberg

Devlin

🌀 "I remember we had a real conversation about whether or not it made sense for Devlin to have that cake! If he was trapped in Crystal, why would he have 'Thanks Spyro' on that cake when he was released? Then we stopped and remembered . . . video game!"

—Josh Nadelberg

Darius

Alban

Thor

Alvar

Nevin

"Nevin was another concept design that was shuffled around. He was originally supposed to be Delbin, but we hadn't been taking into account the voices of the dragons. Luckily, we found a new home for this guy in Toasty that matched much better. It also made sense with the way we rethemed Toasty's castle as a little painting gallery to have a painter up there."

—Josh Nadelberg

Nils

PEACE KEEPERS

O "A lot of it was the props that we }
would give them, and also going back
to the original color schemes. There were
particular details in the original dragons
that were small, but we tried to
amplify them, like the way their
eyes would be drawn or
the fins on their heads
might be particular to
the Peace Keepers."

—DEVON CADY-LEE

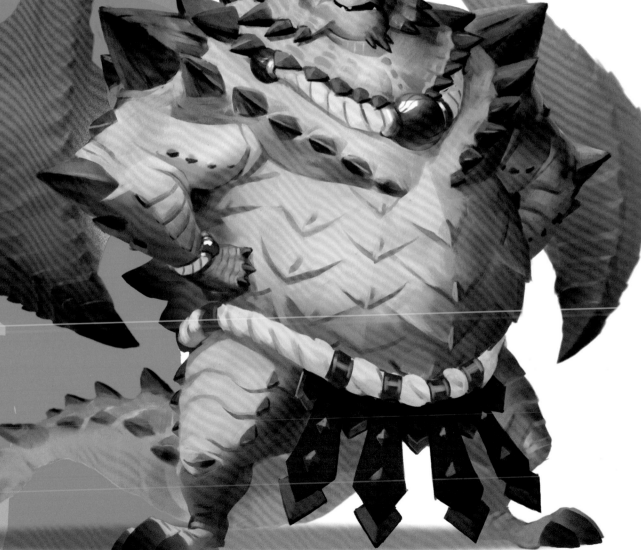

O "The Peace
Keeper dragons
were a huge contrast
with the Artisans. As the
warriors of the Dragon Realms,
we wanted to give them these
big powerful bodies
and details that
made them tough
and rugged."

—JOSH NADELBERG

Trondo

"[Trondo's] got throwing knives, and he looks a little underhanded, but he's big and heroic-looking. He's just rough around the edges."

—Ryan Jones

Marco

"Nick would always pay a lot of attention to the dialogue when he's working. Marco has a secret to share with Spyro, and you can see and feel him leaning in to whisper it in the design."

—Josh Nadelberg

Boris

Conan

Gunnar

Asher

Maximos

Halvor

Ulric

Ivor

"Ivor's original color scheme is basically gray and maybe purple. I tried to retain the same base grayish-purple. He has a bomb, and he has a flying cap. There are little parts of brown that he had in the original, and I tried to use those colors. Instead of using them for horns, I used them for the costume colors." —Devon Cady-Lee

Todor

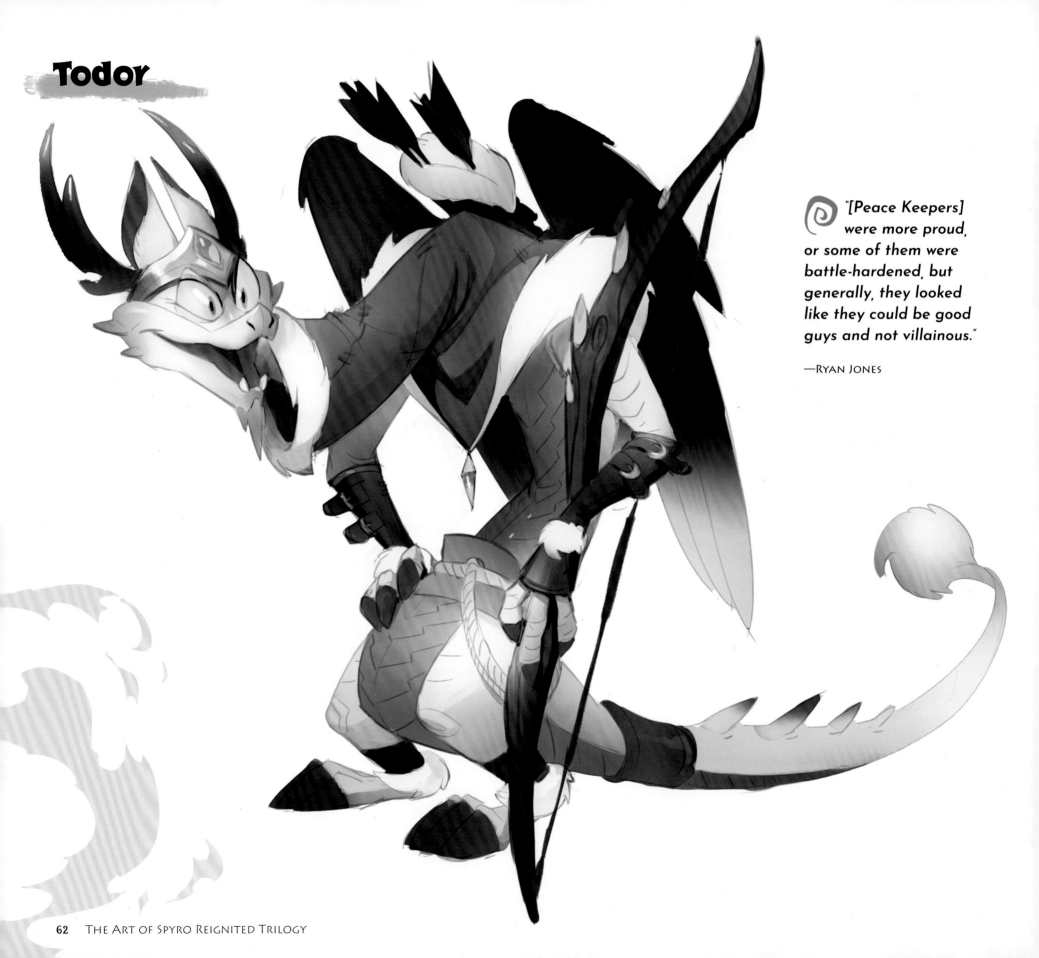

"[Peace Keepers] were more proud, or some of them were battle-hardened, but generally, they looked like they could be good guys and not villainous."

—RYAN JONES

Andor

Ragnar

"Ragnar's concept design was originally intended to be a blacksmith Artisan dragon."

—JOSH NADELBERG

Enzo

"This one (dragon) I designed, his function was a little ambiguous and so was his body type, so I interpreted it one way, and then Josh was like, 'That's cool. I think we might be able to use something like that for another dragon; let me shift it there. But I have an idea for this guy.' So we brainstormed another version and we were able to roll off of my wacky interpretation of that dragon, use it for another one, adjust it, of course, and then pursue another track for this guy that just fit more in line with the gameplay purposes."

—RYAN JONES

MAGIC CRAFTERS

"The Magic Crafters allowed us to lean into some classic fantasy tropes, which was a lot of fun. We wanted them to feel scholarly and a bit uppity, with the occasional mad alchemist thrown into the mix."

—JOSH NADELBERG

"You're only given five or six seconds after those dragons come to life. As concept artists, we were trying to give as much information in our concepts [so] that when it gets passed on to the animators, they can be inspired to take it to the next level."

—JEFF MURCHIE

Lucas

"Nick and Devon used the wings in some really fun and creative ways on the Magic Crafters. Lucas tells Spyro about a secret location, so he's got a treasure map on his wings, and Eldrid was this kooky alchemist with nonsensical formulas scribbled in chalk."

—Josh Nadelberg

Eldrid

Cedric

"Rob's early sketches for Cedric weren't capturing the erudite personality of the Magic Crafters, so we made some tweaks. I do love the shapes in that big old hat he had on."

—Josh Nadelberg

Altair

"It was always great fun to see these ideas come to life. We talked about making Altair a seer, and then Devon went off and gave him a crystal ball, a Magic 8-ball, and 3D glasses . . . of course!"

—Josh Nadelberg

Boldar

"In the beginning, we were playing it conservatively with the costumes and really paying attention to the personality of their faces and the way they're standing so that in every situation, you'd have a unique experience."

—JEFF MURCHIE

Zander

DRAGON PERSONALITIES

"I really wanted to make the dragons as rich and full of personality as possible. Early on, we did a bunch of explorations to see how far we could push it, and I remember, one day, Jeff and Devon almost simultaneously just threw bull's-eyes! We had been playing it a bit too safe, and in those two pages, everything started to fall into place. They captured this charming, really approachable, wise, silly, and grand flavor in those faces. That's when we were off to the races."

—JOSH NADELBERG

"It's not a direct style that we were pulling from, but I kept on going back to the early eighties fantasy video games for inspiration. There's something about the way they handled proportions, shape dynamics, the visual language. I was, in the back of my head, tapping into that."

—JEFF MURCHIE

Cyrus

Cosmos

Zane

Zantor

Hexus

 "When Nico started designing dragons, it was like the floodgates opened! He started adding so many accessories and telling all these fun little stories. For Hexus, we originally wanted him to have a real phoenix as a pet, but that was just too much! We turned it into an ornate detail on the top of his staff."

—Josh Nadelberg

Ajax

Jarvis

BEAST MAKERS

Bubba

"The Beast Makers had this larger-than-life quality to them. Their voices had so much character, and we tried to design dragons that could match those big personalities. Bubba with his vengeful enthusiasm . . . Cyprin's laid-back drawl . . . At this point, we'd learned how to complement the voices really well."

—Josh Nadelberg

"The dragons were a tough one, but they were really fun because we could costume them. And finding the right balance of 'Do dragons wear pants? Spyro doesn't wear pants. At what point does it make it weird?' We concluded that they wear loin cloths and belts."

—Nicholas Kole

Cyprin

"Cyprin was really memorable in the original. He appears in this absurd pose, like he's lounging on a bed. Devon spun that idea into this laid-back and relaxed pose. The straw in the mouth was the perfect touch."

—Josh Nadelberg

Damon

Sadiki

Bruno

Cleetus

Claude

Zeke

"Some dragons have unique lines, while a bunch of them just say, 'Thank you for releasing me!' Zeke was one of those dragons, which was kind of a bummer since he has such a unique design. We imagined him hanging out in the swamp so long that the snails started hanging all over him."

—JOSH NADELBERG

Rosco

Isaak

> "Rosco was like a shaman/warlock type. What I try to do is—I come from a clothing background, I did licensed apparel, boys' T-shirts and costumes and stuff for over ten years, so I start thinking about accessories that can help tell that story."
>
> —ROB DUENAS

Jed

"One of the Beast Maker levels is Treetops, and since they're living high up in these giant trees, we started looking at birds as well as reptiles for reference. Jed is kind of like a big toucan iguana dragon! His animation when he flies away is my favorite touch in the game."

—JOSH NADELBERG

"The Dream Weaver dragons were generally all pretty laid-back and chill, sleepy most of the time and dressed in warm, fuzzy, or knitted things that are comfortable to sleep in."

—RYAN JONES

"Dream Weavers were some of the most fun to work on. We started out looking at dreams from many angles. Moon and star motifs, a nighttime cup of tea, pajamas, stockings . . . We racked our brains to think of anything that might be a fun hook for a design."

—JOSH NADELBERG

Lateef

"*(Dream Weavers) were kept more subdued colors, lot of purples and blues, really low-key. The Artisans were more bright and cheerful.*"

—RYAN JONES

Copano

Bakari

Unika

"The inspiration for Unika was lullabies, and Nico took that and ran with it. He turned him into this amazing musical dragon, with his belly patterns inspired by a violin and tuning pegs on his tail. So much creativity!"

—Josh Nadelberg

Revilo

(P) *"We had another Revilo before him and then I remember Devon drew that knitting, rocking guy, and I was like, 'Oh, my God, he would be so perfect in that hallway, just sitting there knitting and rocking, making his giant dragon sock.' I loved that."*

—JOSH NADELBERG

Mudada

"The theme we were working with for Mudada was stuffed animals and nighttime sleeping friends. He has stuffy wings and horns! The first sketch had a stuffed Spyro, I think, but we ended up making it a fairy in the final design."

—JOSH NADELBERG

Useni

Kosoko

"*I wasn't prepared to see dragons in slippers! There were moments when I was worried people would think we were going off the rails, but we were just having a blast designing these characters. The fun comes through!.*"

—Josh Nadelberg

Baruti

Lutalo

"In a character like Baruti, where the character was purple and pink, you'd start off with that, but he had wings, and you would want to mess with different colors on accessories. Then it was a matter of 'Is it brown? Is it teal? Do the colors match the archetype of the character?'"

—Rob Duenas

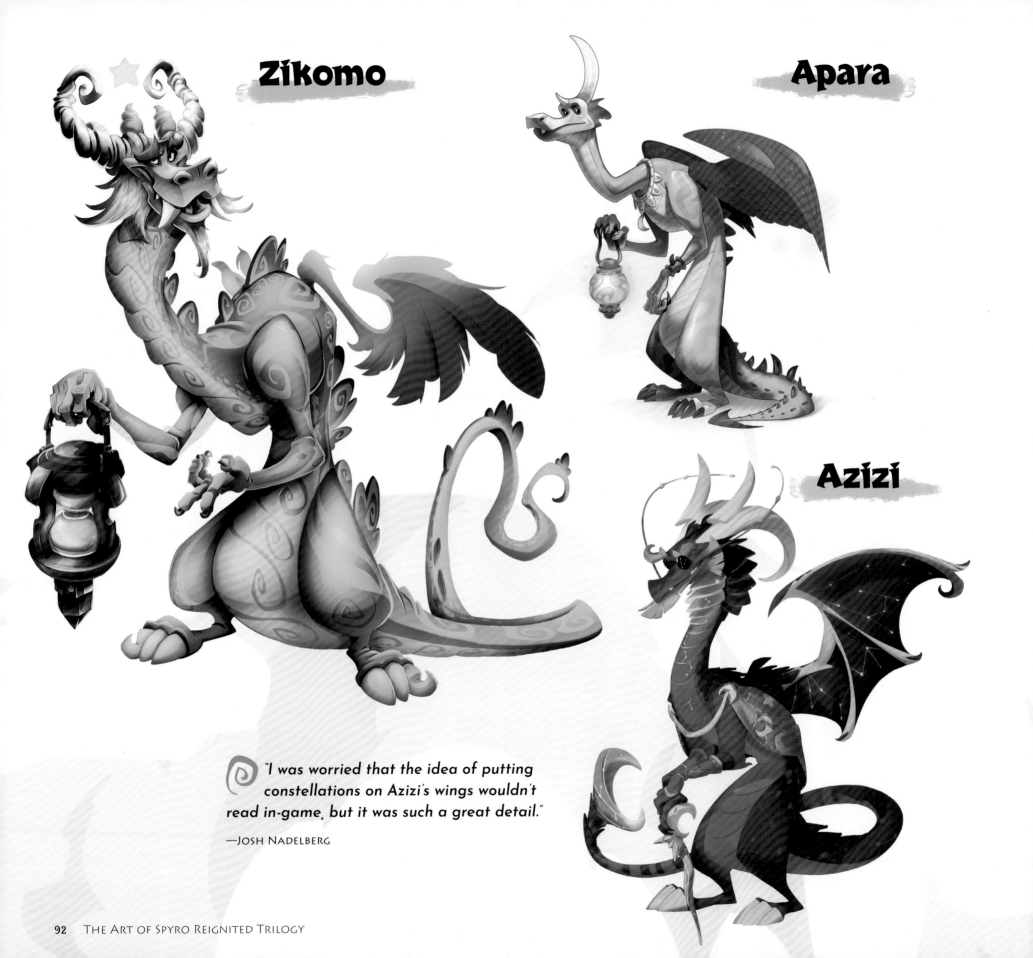

Zikomo

Apara

Azizi

"I was worried that the idea of putting constellations on Azizi's wings wouldn't read in-game, but it was such a great detail."

—Josh Nadelberg

Kasiya

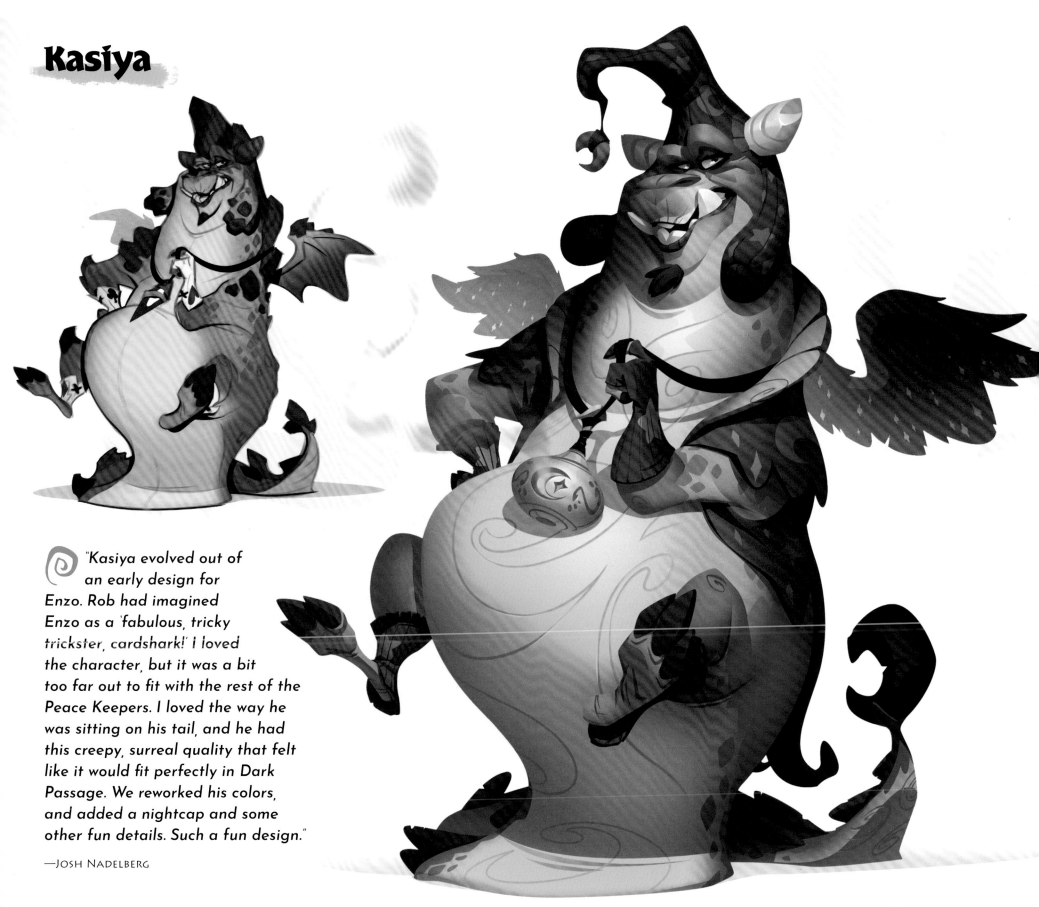

"Kasiya evolved out of an early design for Enzo. Rob had imagined Enzo as a 'fabulous, tricky trickster, cardshark!' I loved the character, but it was a bit too far out to fit with the rest of the Peace Keepers. I loved the way he was sitting on his tail, and he had this creepy, surreal quality that felt like it would fit perfectly in Dark Passage. We reworked his colors, and added a nightcap and some other fun details. Such a fun design."

—JOSH NADELBERG

Friends & Enemies

"I was a big fan from my childhood. My sister and I used to play the game and pass the controller back and forth. The quiet, meditative energy of the whole thing, it was really easy for me to tap into that." —NICHOLAS KOLE

Animal or vegetable?

Remember those heroes and villains we talked about a few chapters ago? Despite encountering some challenges, the artists working on them had fairly clear-cut characters with established stories to start from, an advantage that would not be enjoyed by artists charged with tackling the first three games' kooky cast of supporting creatures.

In the original games, due to the confines of '90s tech and limited disk space, the nonessential characters were given few polygons, and oftentimes, similar base models and shapes were used for multiple critters, with only a color shift to differentiate them.

Toys For Bob's meetings with the original game's developers, Insomniac, provided guidance on the history of the original, including game design docs and original sketches. The studio confirmed, however, that back in the '90s, they had used whatever they had to work with at the time and that they had been moving fast. According to Toys For Bob studio head Paul Yan:

"A lot of it was, 'Hey, we were just developing by the seat of our pants. There was one artist generating models with no real direction, and we were just tossing them into the game.' There's something really fun about how quickly they were developing things and how they were just trying things. It was the '90s, right?"

All of these elements combined meant that a fair amount of the game's nonspeaking role characters didn't even have a clear designation, much less a backstory. Since part of the illustrator's job is to convey story through the art, the team was essentially tasked with telling stories that hadn't been detailed before, a challenge that was eloquently stated in the words of concept artist Ryan Jones:

"How can we make these enemies that are obstacles to you finishing the story be appealing and fit into the world and have an implied backstory? We want them to all feel alive."

Watch me pull a Gnorc outta my hat

So how did those concept artists work their magic?

The team started off with what might be considered low-hanging fruit: Gnorcs and the Balloonist. Gnorcs were the primary antagonists of game one, under the diabolical direction of the aptly named Gnasty Gnorc. While the Gnorcs provided a springboard, their design wasn't completely cut-and-dried. According to concept artist Nicholas Kole,

"A green gnomish-goblin character, you can interpret that in all kinds of ways, even based on those original models. There are a lot of ways you can spin that, so every artist took a

pass, and between me and Nico [Saviori] we honed in on our basic Gnorc."

Art director Josh Nadelberg wanted to make every Gnorc (and every character in the game, for that matter) feel as unique as possible. Part of the problem became clarifying what was a Gnorc and what wasn't. In Josh's words,

"In Gnasty Gnorc's world, there are these dock workers that are supposed to be Gnorcs, but it looks like in the original game they were using the model for the Balloonist, and it was something we really struggled with. We were like, 'It doesn't really make sense that you would have Balloonists. Maybe they're enslaved, maybe Gnasty Gnorc turned them into his minions somehow, because everyone else in the level is a Gnorc, but these guys are pink, and their body shape looks more like the Balloonist.' Eventually, I was like, 'I think we just need to make them Gnorcs.' So we made the decision to make them green, make them Gnorcs, and I remember when we went to Insomniac, I was like, 'Is this what you intended?' and they're like, 'Yeah, they should be Gnorcs!'"

Meanwhile, the real Balloonist character was being contemplated by Nicholas Kole:

"He's a mysterious character, and I remember him very vividly from my childhood, wrapped thickly in a scarf and taking a balloon off into the middle of nowhere. I wanted to know more about that character. Is he human? A critter of some sort?"

The process of nailing down the Gnorcs' and, especially, the Balloonist's design helped to clearly define the tone and style of the rest of the game. Again from Nicholas Kole:

"The Balloonist was a good design for us to determine how much detail and high-fantasy texture we wanted to add to the character. It was with that design, I think, that we really started to establish [that] simpler is better. Really clean, classic. In my mind always is this idea that Spyro is this timeless mascot design, and I wanted all the designs to feel as timeless as I could achieve."

What about the high-hanging fruit?

Creating a full-blown cast of fully realized supporting characters required a little bit of detective work and a whole lot of imagination. The first step was to use as many clues as possible from the original games: What worked? What didn't? What did the vocal performances have to say about the characters' personalities? How did they interact with other characters in the world? What was each one's role in the game? How did the environment affect each identity and personality?

To ensure that the concepts stayed on brand, artists followed the guidelines laid down in Josh's art bible, including:

• Art must possess charm, have a pleasing design, and exhibit simplicity, communication, and magnetism.
• Details must be emotionally expressive and possess a clear indication of personality and an inner life.
• Style appeals to an older audience but is still kid-friendly.
• Designs will push playfulness and personality to the limits.
• Characters should stand out from the environments and express their personality through playful and dynamic animations.

Specific attention was paid to shape language as well. Per the art bible, "Extreme shape play will be the glue that binds it all together and defines the style." Among the advice given in this section of the bible:

• Use thick and thin to break up patterns with playful proportions.
• Oversized features enhance character and push personality.
• Large, playful shapes take priority over accurate anatomy.

Even with the specific art direction, modifying the colorful cast of Spyro was an exploratory process that required a good deal of iteration. In fact, it wasn't uncommon for characters to go through as many as fifteen passes before landing on a final design.

pyro the Dragon

d
builds ... warm ...
it toge ... we w ...
to be gr ... ue bu ... uppe ... ng,
scary and funny. The ... oal was for
a pla ... who played th ... original
... l familiari ...
... rise ... ur inter ...

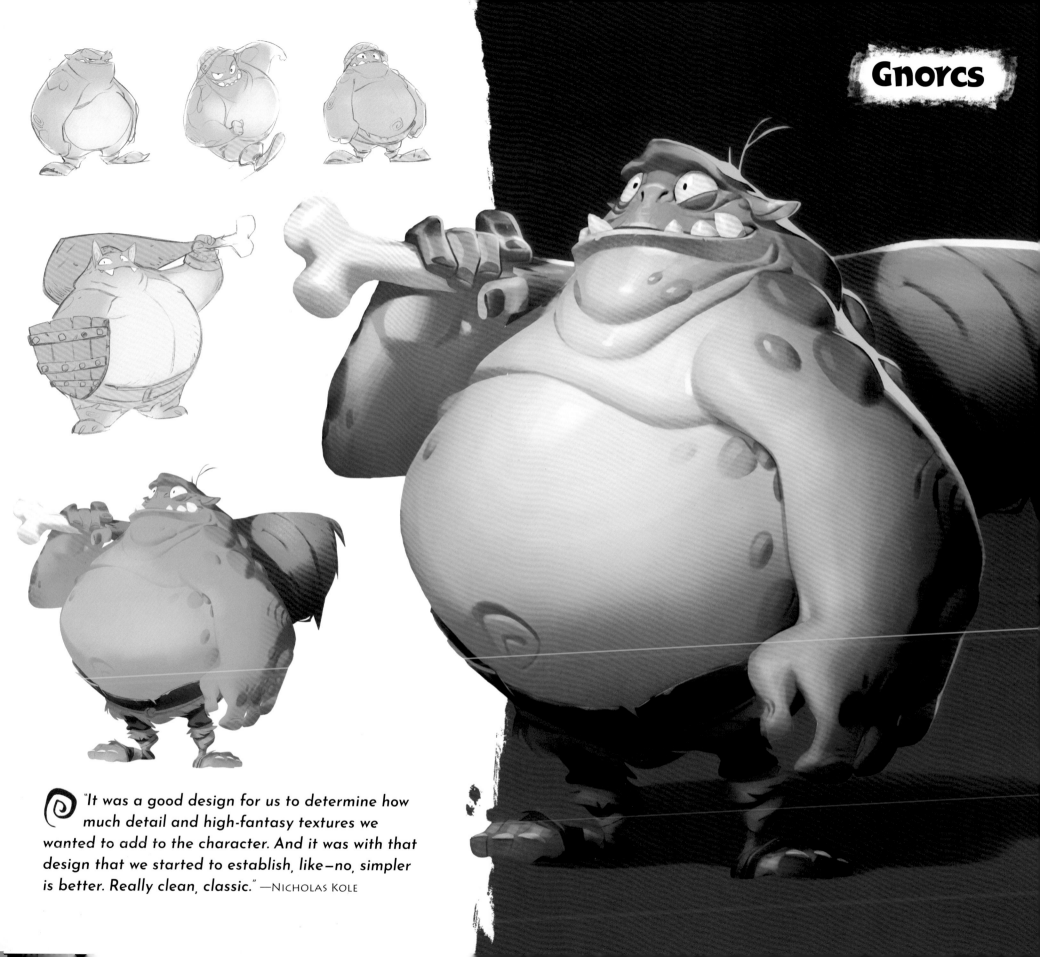

Gnorcs

"It was a good design for us to determine how much detail and high-fantasy textures we wanted to add to the character. And it was with that design that we started to establish, like—no, simpler is better. Really clean, classic." —NICHOLAS KOLE

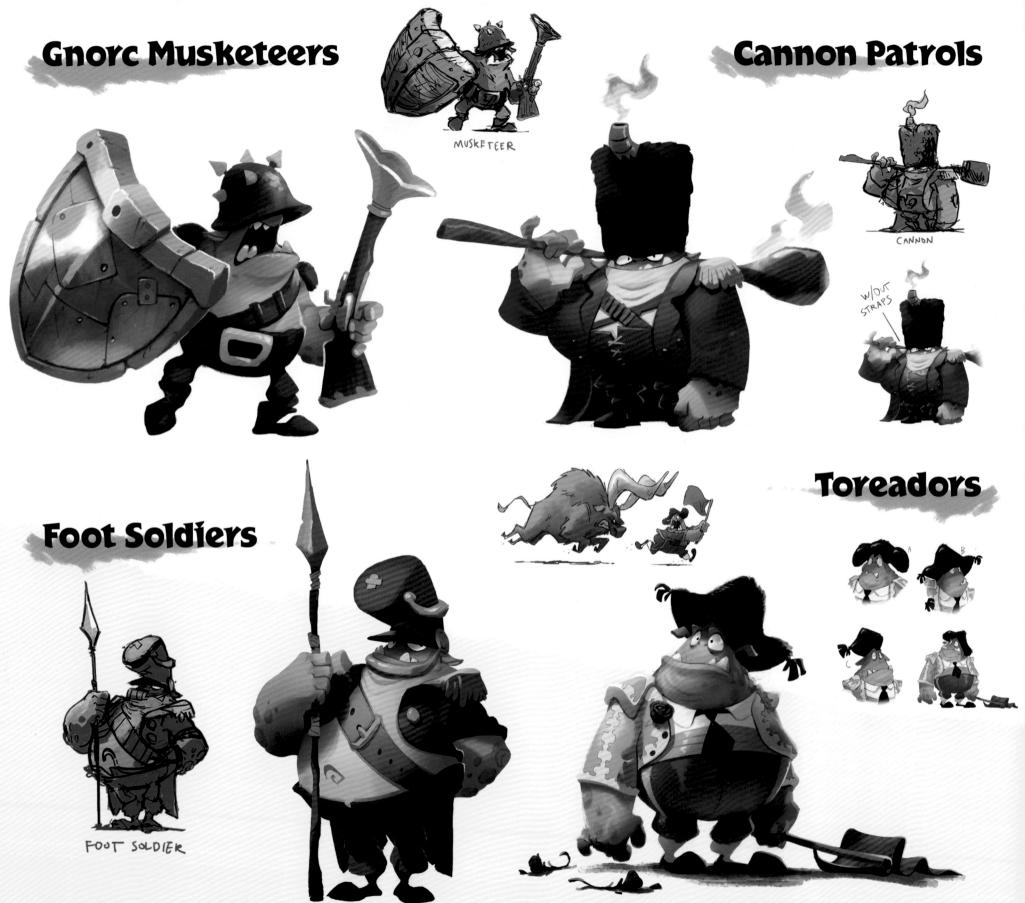

Gnorc Musketeers

MUSKETEER

Cannon Patrols

CANNON

W/OUT STRAPS

Foot Soldiers

FOOT SOLDIER

Toreadors

Balloonist Gnorcs

Gnorc Warriors

🌀 *"Similar to the dragons, we wanted each of the different types of Gnorc to have a distinct personality and character. We didn't want to just play dress up with them."*

—JOSH NADELBERG

Gnorc-Adiers

Gunners

Gnorc Dudes

Electric Gnorcs

Laser Gnorcs

Armored Gnorcs

Snow Gnorcs

Ski Patrols

"I can quickly blob in tons of accessories. There was a total rocker version of the Laser Gnorc; there was a biker type. If I start to see the same character repeating, then I'll go and dig up reference items, and I'll create an accessory list, and then I'll take those accessories and start to layer them onto the characters."

—Rob Duenas

Gnorc Commandos

Gnorc Survivalists

Gnorc Gunners

🌀 "John [Loren] worked on all the Gnorcs in Twilight Harbor, and they're all such great designs. He pushed the shapes in the bodies further than anyone. I remember before we went to model with the survivalist, we weren't sure if he needed eyes under his bandana. I think the animators decided they wanted him to peek out from under there, so we made sure to include them just in case."

—JOSH NADELBERG

🌀 "We decided to replace the realistic machine guns with these awesome rotary goo blasters. It felt more in line with the tone of the game and was more colorful and dynamic."

—JOSH NADELBERG

Gem Thieves

Gold tooth!

Green & Elder Wizards

"There were a bunch of characters that were more ambiguous than others as we started to reimagine them. What were these wizards? We didn't think they were human, so we decided to make them these mysterious, dark, cosmic forms under their robes."

—Josh Nadelberg

Egg Thieves

"To this day, when I'm drawing, I leave on long plays of Spyro and all those '90s games, mostly to keep myself motivated."

—Rob Duenas

Sleeping Dogs

"*Toasty was the level we selected for our first prototype, so we worked on the sleeping dogs right out of the gate. We wanted to bring out as much personality as possible, and I remember Nico did this great page of sketches with all of these ideas for how he could animate. When I saw the little sketch of him raising one eye and peering around, I was sold on the design.*"

—Josh Nadelberg

Sheep

Boars

Armored Turtles

> *"The visual storytelling is still there. It's not as in-depth as the dragons, with the visual narratives happening on them that's very elaborate. With the enemies, it's much more up front and surface, and you have to be clear and precise when presenting them."*

—Jeremy Anninos

Beasts

Bulls

Fools

"The fools in Dream Weaver were a real challenge. In the original, they were these bizarre simple shapes, and we wanted to capture the absurdity of them without making them too creepy or too cute. Nico really threaded the needle on those guys."

—JOSH NADELBERG

BOM!

NOSE?

Armored Horrors

KIND OF HANDS

LIKE A CRAB

A

B

C

D

LONG CLAWS

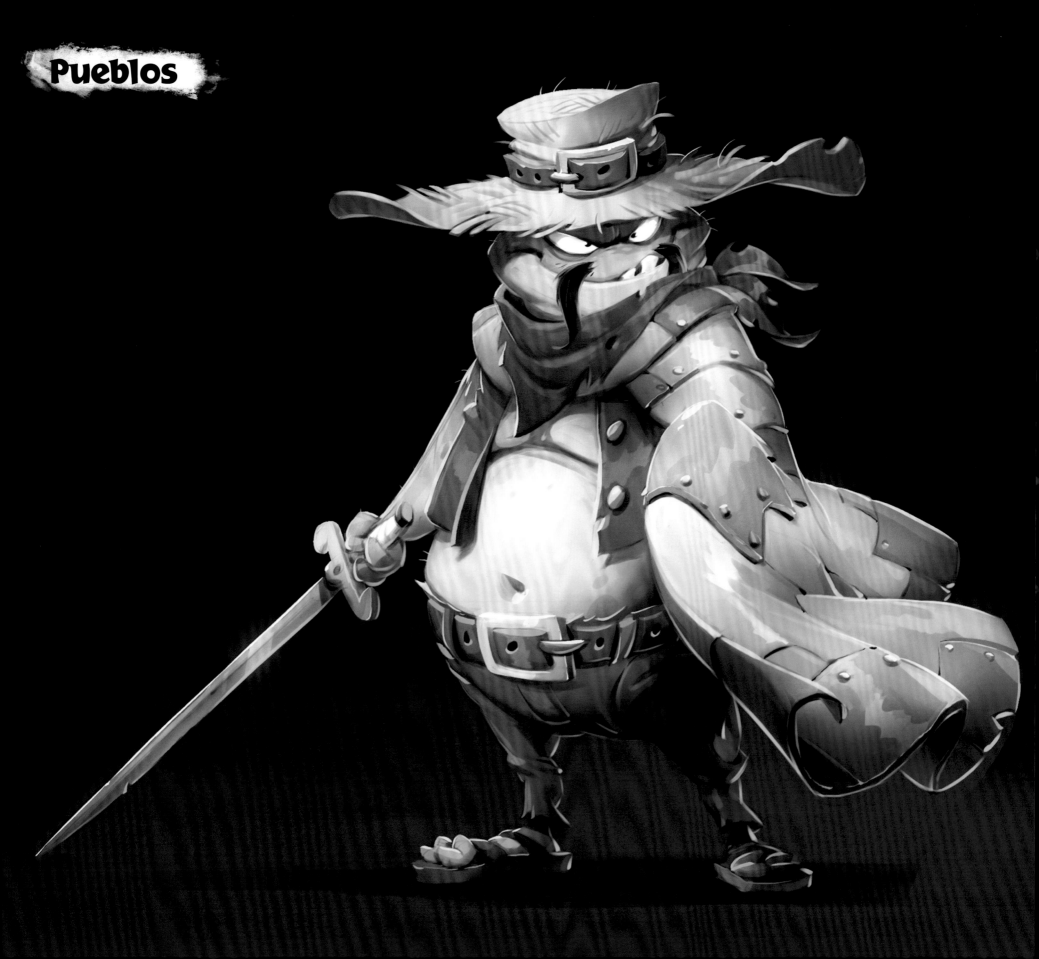

Pueblos

Druids

"The druids were another bunch of characters that we weren't quite sure what to do with. They were bearded, robed—things? With green hair? Were those noses or beaks? Were they birds? We really weren't sure how to translate them. Oleg had a lot of fun figuring it out, and we laughed a lot at his explorations."

—Josh Nadelberg

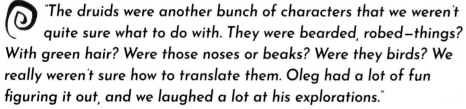

HUMAN

or

SPIRIT   PUFF!

JOHN TAICHI

DRUID exploration

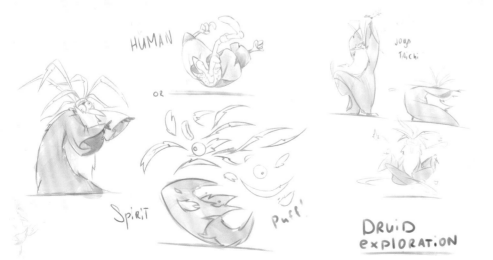

What are you?!

shepherd   same reel size   old druid

Demon Dogs

"In the original game, the baby demon dog looked like a cute little puppy. We have dogs all over the studio at Toys For Bob and didn't want Spyro burning puppies! We decided to make him a quirky little bulldog. Early versions of the monster form were losing the crazy lamprey-shaped mouth, so we tried to work that back into the design."

—Josh Nadelberg

Cupids

Banana Boys & Strongarms

"For the enemies, a lot of the personality has to be there in the first read, and by a glimpse of the character's shape or what they're wearing, you have to tell what they're about."

—JEREMY ANNINOS

STRONGARMS

"*The banana boys required a fair amount of interpretation. John came up with a fun take, and when we got to the armored version, I remember there were a few ideas kicking around. We all thought the bucket head was the most fun.*"

—Josh Nadelberg

Friends & Enemies
Spyro 2: Ripto's Rage

Moneybags

🌀 "[Moneybags] was a big one that was vocally driven. So I had to capture that smug quality that he has, and that also is informed by your feelings after the fact, about Moneybags. We wanted to create an even more despicable interpretation of him."

—Nicholas Kole

Bombo

Riflemen

Guards

Gemcutters

Colossus Yeti

Zoe

Robot Gulp

Robot Pterodactyl

"In the final boss battle, Ripto rides a robotic version of Gulp and then swoops around on this big robotic pterodactyl. Nico made these great steampunk designs for them. It's amazing to think about how much energy goes into each of these characters that has just a moment or two of gameplay!"

—JOSH NADELBERG

Breezebuilders

Land Blubbers

Private Romeo

"Zephyr and Breezebuilder Harbor are all about the conflict between the Land Blubbers and the Breezebuilders. Ryan came up with a great design for the Land Blubbers and decked them out in some great accessories. The military guys had tuna-can hats and rubber duckie staffs. He made every detail really fun and creative."

—JOSH NADELBERG

Satyrs

The Alchemist

Fauns

The Mayor

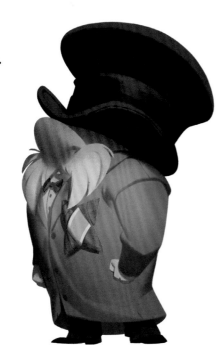

Basil the Explorer

Serpents

"In the original game, the Mayor and Basil were very similar in shape, so we wanted to honor that in the redesigns of these characters."

—JOSH NADELBERG

Gear Grinder Thieves

Gear Grinders

ANTI-ACCIDENT HELMET?

NECKLACE?

PATCH BEHIND HIS JACKET

Gear Grinder Robots

Armed Thieves

Shielded Armed Thieves

"His shield is more of a monochromatic thing that pops out in a very colorful world, so you know to avoid it and hit his colorful, soft body. You want to avoid their swords, so their swords are also called out. I didn't go so far as to make them red, but they were definitely one of the lightest parts of the design."

—RYAN JONES

Genies

Shady Oasis Thieves

"They were just, like, little guys with turbans and robes and eyes, and very low-poly. Josh gave me free rein to come up with a backstory in my head and try to solidify what was very much abstract."

—RYAN JONES

Ice Wizards

Lava Lizards

MELT

Bee Trees

Killer Bushes

Earthshapers

Warlocks

Agent Zero

George

Handel & Greta

"The second game had all of these crazy stories in each of the levels. In Scorch, these two kids have been kidnapped, but it turns out they're really secret agents with red laser eyes! It is some really wild stuff! Nico came up with some great designs for the kids. Greta looks like she could secretly be a spy. Not so sure about Handel."

—Josh Nadelberg

Queen Finny

Dolphin Spectators

Fish Spectators

Sunny Beach Turtles

Capybaras

"The second game had so many wild characters. There are Capybaras driving motorboats and race cars. I would have loved to be around when they came up with some of these ideas!"

—Josh Nadelberg

Oxen

Yaks

Camels

Goats

Farmer Applebee

FODDER

"As if there wasn't enough to redesign, there are tons of little critters littered throughout the game as fodder for Spyro to burn and turn into butterflies for Sparx to gobble. While they were simpler to implement than other enemies, we still gave each of them a facelift."

—Josh Nadelberg

"That was one of the things about upscaling and raising the fidelity of these characters. A lot of the old characters are a few polygons and one or two colors. So building them from the ground up to high resolution quality is a big part of adding tertiary colors."

—Jeremy Anninos

Friends & Enemies
Spyro: Year of the Dragon

🌀 *"Like the Gnorcs in the first game, there were tons of Rhynocs in Year of the Dragon. We wound up using just a few base Rhynoc designs and then dressed them up in accessories and different outfits to tell their stories. This allowed us to share animations and get through all of them efficiently.*

—JOSH NADELBERG

Rhynocs

Rhynocs

"One of the things I'm most excited about every day working with the team here is the amount of character and expression and creativity that they bring out through the character designs, the models, the animations—everything. It all comes together in a super playful and charming way."

—JOSH NADELBERG

Crazy Ed

Egyptian Dogs

Farley

RHYNOC BALL

"You're not reimagining the game itself; you're reimagining the look of the game to create something new from the ground up."

—Ryan Jones

Bartholomew

Dino Mines Rabbits

⟳ *"To help bring some more character to Bartholomew we gave him oversized untied sneakers and a phone. He thinks he's too cool for school."*

—Josh Nadelberg

Country Speedway Cows

Fireflies

Oleg didn't have a gaming console during his childhood. While working on the project, he would wake up every day and watch long plays of the original Spyro before drawing. "The funniest part," he said, "was that I got nostalgia when Spyro Reignited Trilogy was released."

Motorboat Bears

Sunrise Spring Lions

COOLER

Blue Flies

Flying Beavers

Crystal Flowers

Bumblebees

Butterflies

WITHOUT EYE GLOW

Baby Dragons

"We figured we didn't have to put nearly as much variety into the baby dragons as we did with the adults. Babies kind of all look alike, right? We wound up having three different body types and stayed pretty true to the tone of the original."

—JOSH NADELBERG

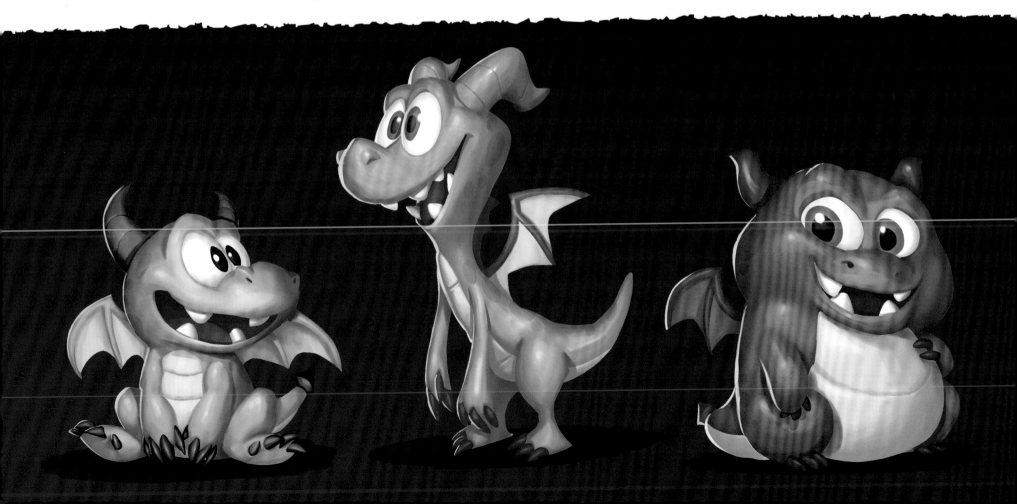

The World of Spyro

⌖ "Stay true to the spirit of the original levels but also feel free to interpret them in our own way. Add in our own depth and environmental storytelling where appropriate. Make the environments feel fun, playful, and full of character."

—BILLY WIMBLETT

Activate the Spyroscope!

As the Toys For Bob team jumped into development on Spyro Reignited Trilogy, one of their first goals was to analyze as much data as they could from the original metrics of the game. While a meeting with Insomniac provided some early guidance, most of the metrics data were meticulously indexed by TFB's QA team.

So, as it dove into classic Spyro and began the task of cataloguing everything in the game, a brave and, no doubt, caffeine-augmented engineer set about creating a tool to help the process . . . Spyroscope! This modern marvel's technological wizardry helped the team to rebuild the game from the ground up.

With the foundation they needed to get started, the environment artists were ready to begin working on a creation faithful to the spirit of the hundred-plus—yep, you read that right—levels from the original three games.

Embrace the wonk!

"Make it crazy, wonky, and super fun!" That was the direction given to all the artists on the project by art director Josh Nadelberg. Now, you might be asking yourself, "What does 'wonky' even mean?" Well, that's where we come back around to that trusty art bible!

Among the helpful rules established in the bible: "Stay true to the spirit of the original: Capture the magic of what it was like to play Spyro for the first time," "Push playfulness and personality to the limits," and—you may remember this one from the Friends & Enemies intro— "Extreme shape play will be the glue that binds it all together and defines the style."

For shape language, especially, visual examples were provided along with specific instruction to avoid parallel lines, right angles, and even spacing as well as staying away from repetition of scale and placement. Also, in the example of looking at a wall, shapes on the bottom or closer to the ground would be larger in size and then decrease as you look up, giving the wall a grander feel.

Light reading

The art bible described rules for lighting within the game, encouraging creatives to think of light as the most "important artistic weapon" in their arsenal. Emphasis was placed on rich moods and atmosphere. The team was encouraged to "not feel constrained by real-world rules, and to use light as a way to bring magic and life to the scenes."

It's (not) all in the details

Another guiding principle found in the art bible concerned detail. How much is too much? Per the bible: "Avoid high frequency details and noise in materials and textures," and "Add details that help express character and enhance the design." Specific attention was given to how rock and wood textures should look. The overall theme was to avoid too much detail and to not have overly glossy or chrome-like surfaces.

Yeah but what about the wonk? You told me to embrace the wonk!

Right. Well, Josh included a very helpful visual example in the art bible, reproduced here for your viewing pleasure.

WONKY!

NOT WONKY!

Stay on target!

Having to color inside the lines of the original game seems like it could be restricting for the artists, right? Well, it was and it wasn't. The helpful folks at Insomniac did provide some useful guidelines regarding levels, including: "Color should convey an emotional journey from level to level"; "Each level, or area in a level, should have a core color palette of two to three colors"; and "Color shading adds to the richness of the world." But, as Josh noted in the art bible, "There's a huge opening for us to add texture and flavor to the levels." So what was it like to try and stay faithful to the spirit of classic Spyro while still interpreting and exploring the artists' own expressions? Lead concept artist Ron Kee described it thusly:

> "There are so many fantastic ideas, and sometimes you get really inspired and you might just put your music on and start drawing, and all of a sudden, before you know it, what you've drawn has totally morphed into something completely different than the original, and it might look really cool but then you have to take a couple steps back."

Okay, so it sounds like a real balancing act. Which it was. Some of the restrictions that came with remastering the original levels included not altering the bounding boxes or collision of the geometry for pathable/playable areas, meaning— for those who aren't fluent in video game lingo— that there were parts of the maps that Spyro could

interact with and explore in the original and parts he couldn't. And that needed to stay the same for Spyro Reignited Trilogy.

The real freedom for artists came from the fact that the poly count wasn't nearly as big of a problem in Spyro Reignited Trilogy as it was back in 1998 for classic Spyro. According to studio head Paul Yan:

> "On the art side of things, there was a huge opportunity for us—twenty years have passed. Not only is it uprezzing what's there but also filling in the details and suggestions that we were seeing in the game. For example, the floor was covered in grass, but they weren't able to render individual blades of grass or make them interactive, so that seemed like a technical improvement that we could do."

The higher poly budget also meant that artists could engage in more storytelling through the environment. Examples of this included everything from using banners that signified Gnorcish rule in game one, *Spyro the Dragon*, to a room in Zephyr from *Spyro 2: Ripto's Rage* that represented the metamorphosis of a caterpillar to a butterfly.

Resources, however, were not inexhaustible, and this was particularly stress-tested in the level Dragon Shores, where an overly ambitious dragon rollercoaster almost didn't make the cut. In the end, however, the coaster stayed in. Why?

Probably because it was crazy, wonky, and super fun.

Dragon Realms
Spyro the Dragon

🌀 "Bringing the world of Spyro to life required just as much work as all of the characters. Between the three games, there were about a hundred different environments, and we wanted to give them the same amount of love by taking ideas and inspiration from the originals and adding details and flavor to enhance the storytelling and the mood."

—JOSH NADELBERG

ARTISANS HOMEWORLD

 "Sometimes we tried to be very faithful. In the Artisan world, we tried to be very accurate to the spirit of the original. And in some other levels, we were more liberal, where we just took the base that was there, we looked into the story they developed for that world, and then tried to enhance it."

—Johannes Figlhuber

 "No other level needed to nail that feeling of coming home like Artisans. It needed to feel like a hug. I think we captured the perfect balance of the old and the new so you don't question for a second that these are the Dragon Realms you remembered."

—Josh Nadelberg

Stone Hill

Dark Hollow

 "We played up the library and literary theme in Dark Hollow. The addition of bookshelves and candles made a great home for thespian dragons and poets and scribes."

—Josh Nadelberg

Town Square

 For Ron Kee, the process starts with conversations with the designers "trying to get a sense of what their goal is for the level, as far as gameplay goes, and if there's any narrative to the level. I need to talk to the right people about that as well."

Sunny Flight

Toasty

PEACE KEEPERS HOMEWORLD

@ "The characters are the actual storytellers in the game, but a lot of times, I think people overlook the importance of the environment. The way I look at it, an environment is like a character as well, although it's in the background because you don't want it to compete, but it has to have all the personality to help support all the characters."

—RON KEE

@ "Peace Keeper levels feature these armored battlements and structures in a rocky desert landscape. Ron put so much thought into all of the details. The carvings in the temple in Doctor Shemp's level, the ornamentation on the shields—everything had a purpose."

—JOSH NADELBERG

Dry Canyon

Cliff Town

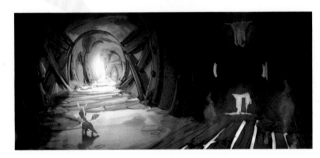

Ice Cavern

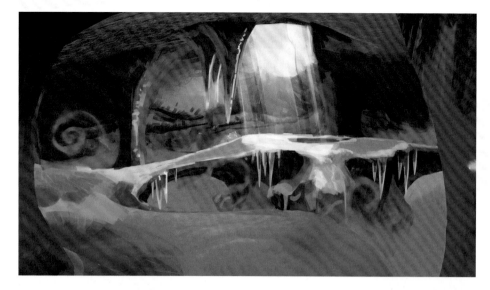

🌀 "We used similar architecture in Ice Cavern as the earlier Peace Keeper levels, but it feels really different with the cool snowy palette. The concept artists added all of the whimsical swirls in the snow, which helped add that storybook charm we were going for."

—Josh Nadelberg

Night Flight

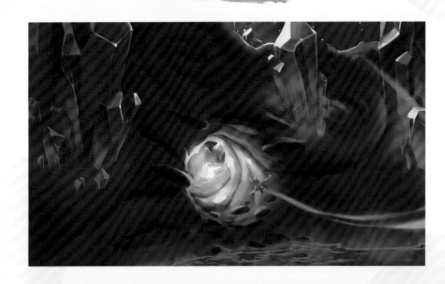

Doctor Shemp

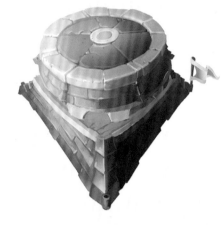

MAGIC CRAFTERS HOMEWORLD

"It was very important to get the areas that were playable and touchable by Spyro as accurate as possible. Game design was very adamant about us keeping the collision authentic. If you could not touch it and could not reach it, we could do whatever we wanted."

—SIMON KOPP

Height difference   Dirt → variety

Shadow outlines to highlight tips

Alpine Ridge

○ "Spyro is an open world game, where you can explore anywhere, so the concept art had to give the 3D artists enough of a feel for the levels that they could improvise and take the visuals and extend them to every inch of the map."

—Josh Nadelberg

High Caves

Wizard Peak

Crystal Flight

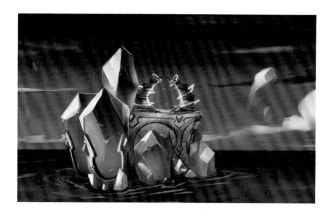

 "We looked at games that had a similar stylistic base, but were more modern than Spyro used to be, and how they solved problems. A lot of Overwatch, of course—how they did surfaces and shaders and proportions."

—Johannes Figlhuber

Blowhard

BEAST MAKERS HOMEWORLD

"One of our main tasks on Spyro was to paint environments in the spirit of the original. Usually, I opened up original 3D files to find a nice camera angle, and I would add lighting intention sometimes and make quick reference screenshots and start building and painting the new environment right away."

—Florian Coudray

Terrace Village

Misty Bog

"We found out that there were some dark or mysterious intentions behind some levels that could not be achieved graphically back in 1998, so we tried to bring those ideas up in the color palette and mood."

—FLORIAN COUDRAY

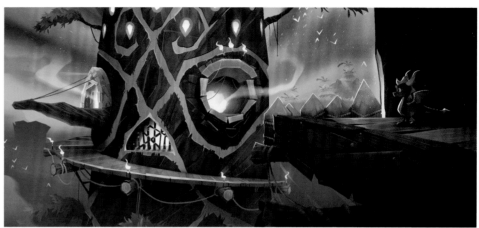

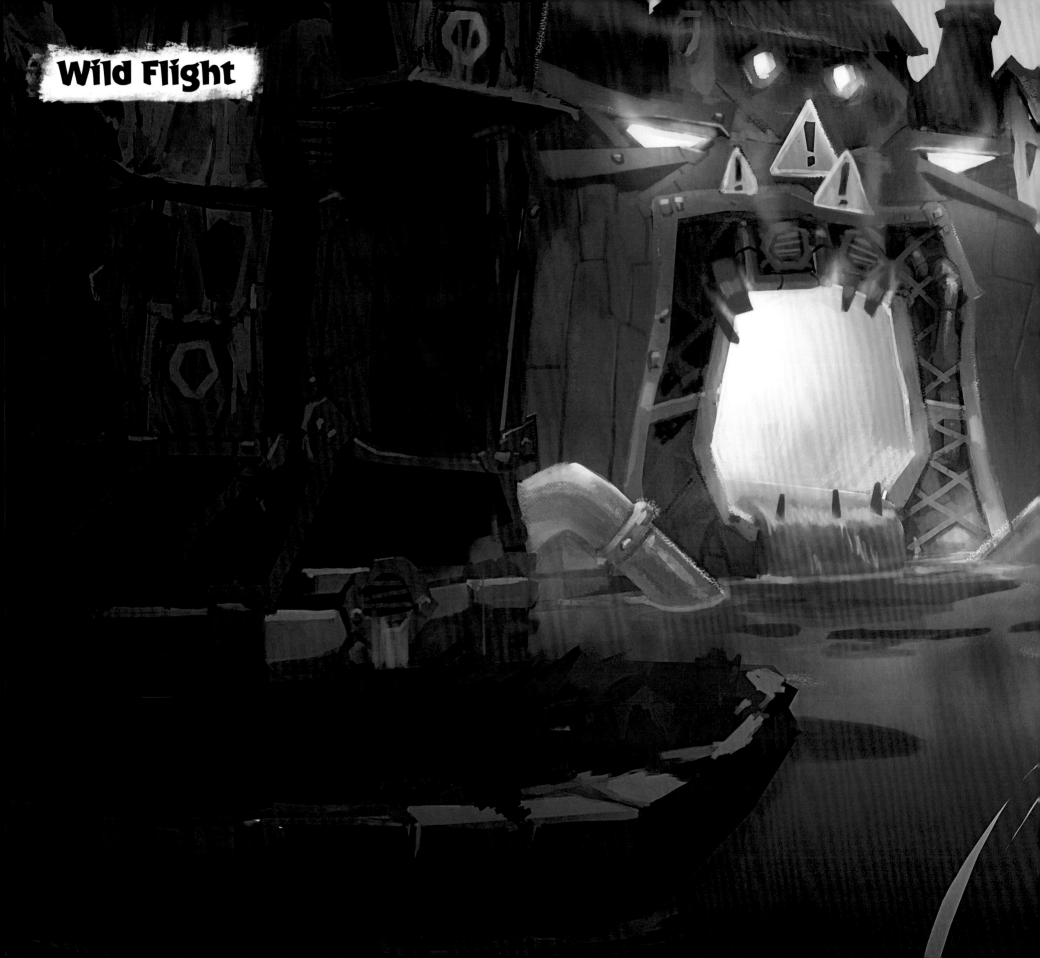

Wild Flight

Metalhead

"We were halfway through production on the 3D environment for Metalhead's level when we realized that Spyro can turn around at the start point, and we had no idea what to put behind him! We quickly painted up a vista with some dead trees and a sunset. It was actually quite a lovely painting."

—JOSH NADELBERG

DREAM WEAVERS HOMEWORLD

"We were encouraged to explore interpretations of the original levels and incorporate new ideas, but at the same time, I knew the more 'out there' I went with my interpretation, the more likely some fans would be disappointed that the level didn't look the way they remembered it, or the way they had imagined it in their heads."

—BILLY WIMBLETT

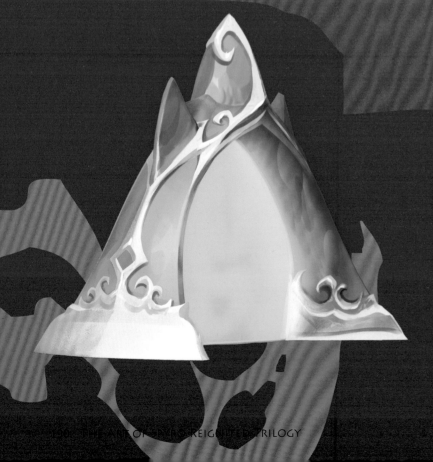

Dark Passage

(Q) "The 'nightmare,' which I came up with as a way of explaining the spooky things happening in Dark Passage, was this seeping, dark influence that corrupts the otherwise dreamlike locations of the Dream Weavers."

—BILLY WIMBLETT

(Q) "I played this up a lot in Dark Passage, designing a melted, twisted look for the rock surfaces and architecture inside the caverns."

—BILLY WIMBLETT

Lofty Castle

 *"There was one image where the castle was floating under a beautiful sunset sky and then the darkness of space below. It captured the magic of the Dream Weavers realm perfectly. Everything had this surreal quality."*

—Josh Nadelberg

Haunted Towers

Icy Flight

Jacques

"I tried not to depart from the original colors too much, but sometimes it either made sense to (such as when updating an environment with more realistic or consistent lighting) or there were just colors I wanted to use for personal aesthetic reasons."

—Billy Wimblett

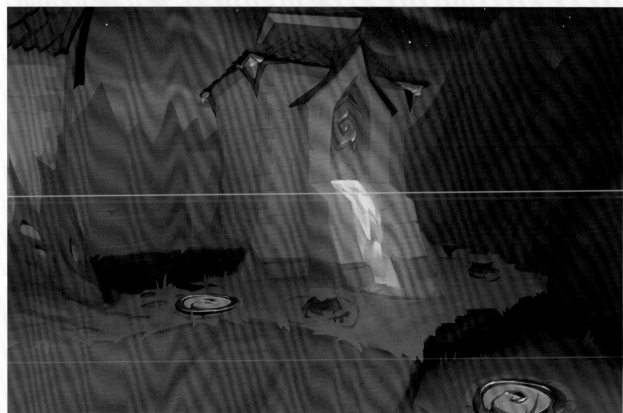

GNASTY'S WORLD

@ *"Sometimes when you have a cool level, you have cool resources to pick from already, but maybe you're trying to define it a little bit more, and sometimes we had to take liberties to push the visuals just a little bit further."*

—RON KEE

Gnorc Cove

"Gnasty Gnorc stuff is a mix of Artisans and very crude mechanics. Let's call it 'coalpunk' because everything has coal and heaters and pipes. That was really fun to do."

—Simon Kopp

Twilight Harbor

> "We stuck basically 100 percent to the color scheme. We tried to stick to the colors in the first game because the first game had great art direction in terms of color, and there wasn't really anything we needed to add."
>
> —SIMON KOPP

Gnasty's Loot

"Simon imagined the final room in Gnasty's Loot as Gnasty's man cave. We used that set for the intro cinematic and put an old beat-up couch in there for him to sit on. In the concept art, we had all of these posters from the original Spyro games on the wall that we thought was kind of a funny gag, but that got nixed at some point. In the back, there was a hidden crystal dragon peeking out from behind some boards. Simon was always coming up with little easter eggs."

—Josh Nadelberg

Avalar
Spyro 2: Ripto's Rage

@ *"In the second game, the environments were even more diverse than the first game and much larger in scale and scope. Almost every level had an entirely new look and feel, which was daunting. In Spyro, all the Peace Keeper levels had a consistent visual language, for example, but in games 2 and 3, it was the Wild West from one world to the next."*

—JOSH NADELBERG

SUMMER FOREST

> "For architecture I try to look up mostly unused environments or architecture styles. For Summer Forest, we took a Turkish bath theme."
>
> —Jakob Eirich

> "I made it a very happy place with these green meadows and blue water. I wanted the player to wish to be there, to spend their vacation in that place."
>
> —Jakob Eirich

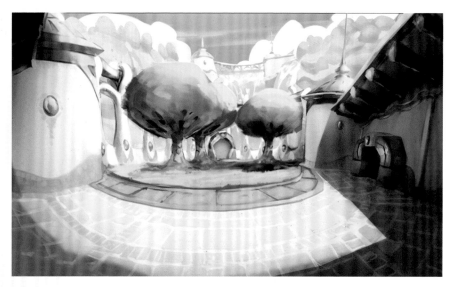

"In Summer Forest, there's this hall right after the starting point. It's a room where the floor dropped down, everything is overgrown, but I couldn't add new geometry to that. It had to be left to the player to imagine that this floor dropped down and that the pieces are somewhere in the ground now." —JAKOB EIRICH

"The play area underneath that upper level could have been streamlined and could have been made more dynamic. I had to make it work with the blocky mesh, which was not convenient but it worked in the end."

—JAKOB EIRICH

The World of Spyro 205

Glimmer

Idol Springs

🌀 This is the first level that has so many playable areas—some of them are underwater, some of them are in the buildings. You have to figure out how to connect the two areas together."

—SERINA MO

🌀 "You have to figure out how to make, say, area seven—some of area seven's buildings are really tall so that you can see them from area two, so you have to figure out how those things play out in your design."

—SERINA MO

Colossus

Sunny Beach

Hurricos

Aquaria Towers

Crush's Dungeon

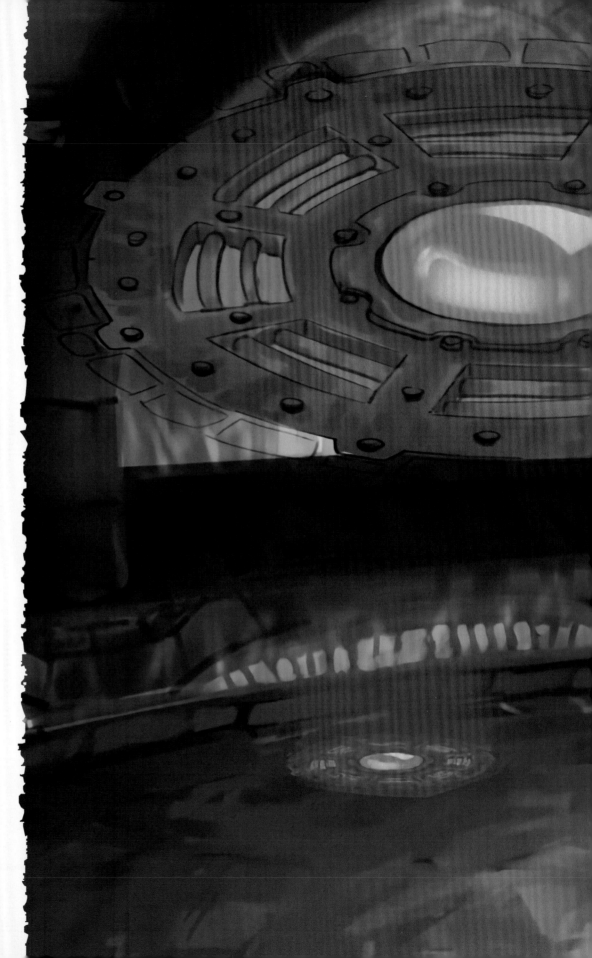

"One time, I misjudged the scaling a lot. It was Crush's Dungeon. The scaling of the base mesh didn't convey the size of the room. It looked smaller than it actually was. When I realized my idea with that room and placed Spyro, the room was way too small."

—JAKOB EIRICH

"There were times when the 3D team would have to solve some problems that we missed in the concepts. We would try to do pickups or paintovers, as they were working to help clarify the intent of the design."

—JOSH NADELBERG

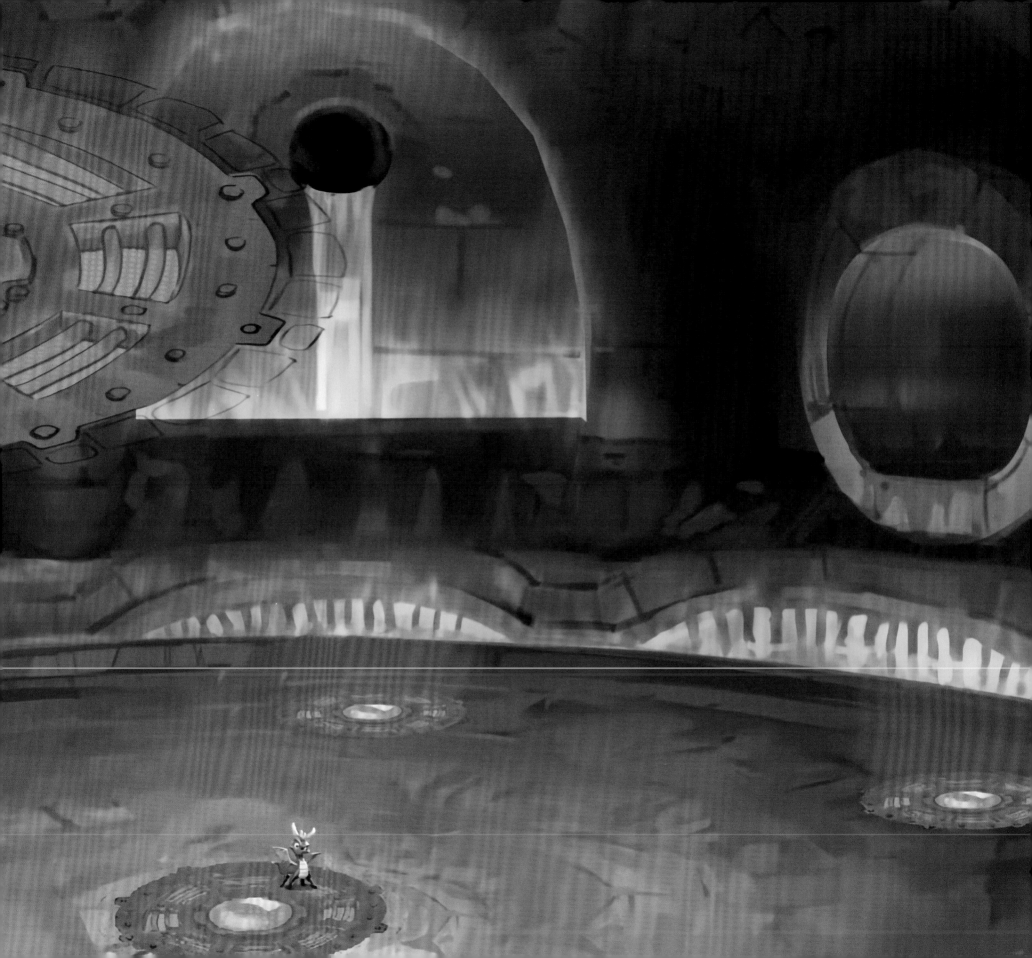

Ocean Speedway

"The speedway levels were challenging because you're zooming through them so fast. We made sure not to overdesign them but still wanted to tell a good visual story. Ocean Speedway had these big structures that felt inspired by the ocean environment. We added a shell motif and dragon scales to them, and it ended up working really well."

—JOSH NADELBERG

AUTUMN PLAINS

"Some levels seemed to resonate with the fans more than others. We knew Autumn Plains needed to really transport the player and trigger all of those strong memories. We made sure to get the mood and the lighting just right."

—Josh Nadelberg

Skelos Badlands

Crystal Glacier

Breeze Harbor

"There's also, in this level, one little boat which has a sail out of dragon skin. Also, as I said, they are military-looking birds. I tried to put this military element into the level, so I topped the buildings with a roofing that looks like a grenade. These little details I tried to implement to support their backstory."

—Jakob Eirich

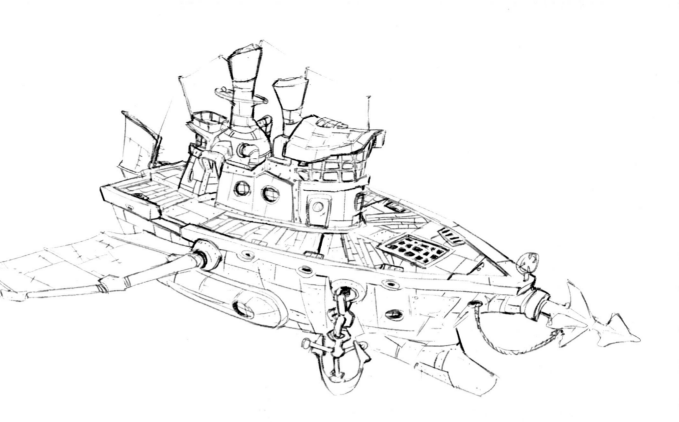

Zephyr

"I really liked Zephyr. We changed how things look quite a lot. It made way more sense for the story that these Land Blubber caterpillar worms would live in an environment that was more natural."

—Johannes Figlhuber

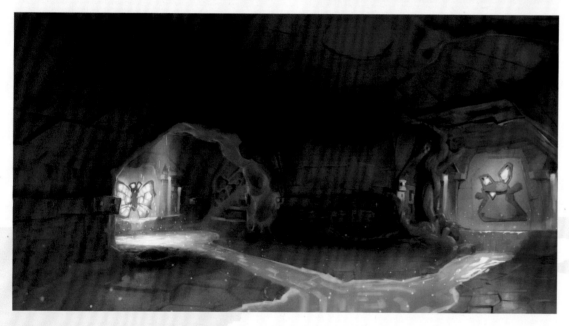

"I designed one underground room that is basically—I think that no one gets it, ever, but that room is designed to show the evolution of the caterpillar to their final state of being a butterfly."

—Simon Kopp

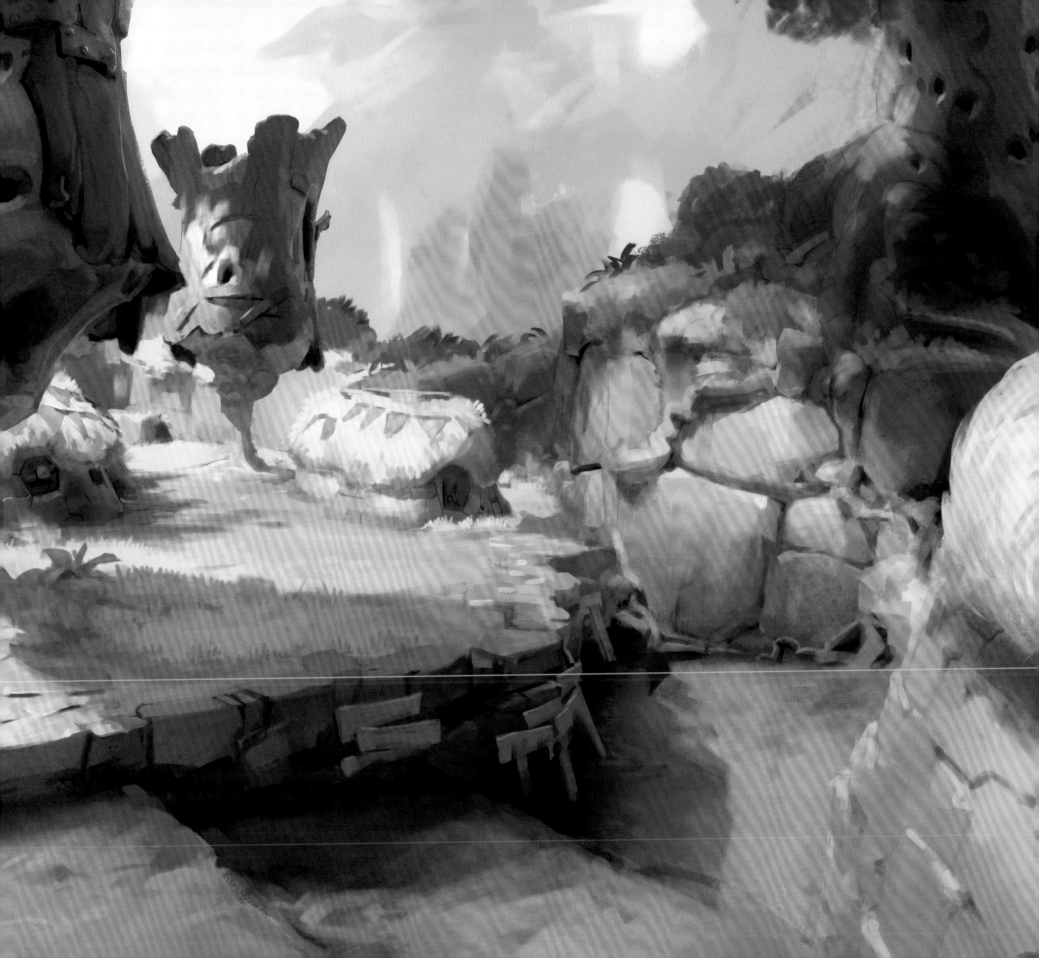

Scorch

Fracture Hills

"For the original game [Fracture Hills is] just walls. There's nothing else. My challenge was to figure out how to make those areas look interesting, but at the same time, the player knows they cannot access those areas."

—SERINA MO

"The characters in there blow in a horn to make music, so I started to implement the horn shape into the design."

—SERINA MO

Magma Cone

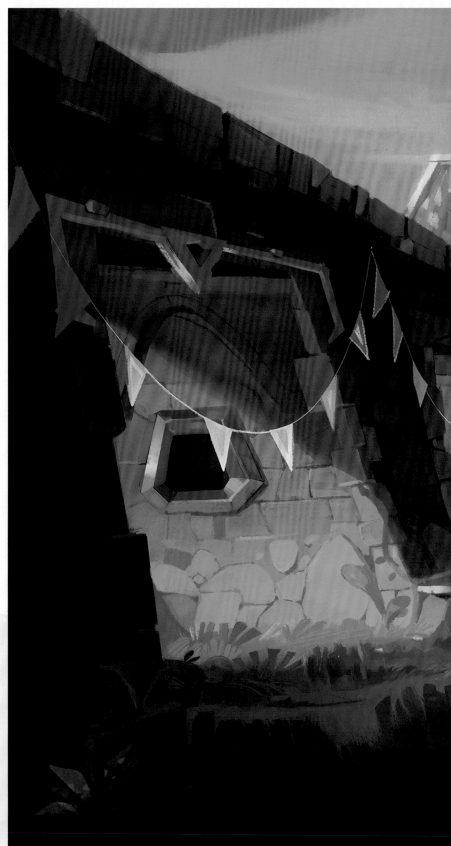

Shady Oasis

"The biggest restriction by far was the requirement not to noticeably interfere with the collision of the levels. It was a sometimes frustrating, but ultimately necessary, requirement to keep the experience consistent with that of the original game."

—Billy Wimblett

Icy Speedway

"Min [Fu] captured a beautiful sunset in her concepts for Icy Speedway. It was a challenge to replicate that in the game, but at the end of the day, I think this level came together beautifully. Having beautiful concept art really inspires the 3D artists to push themselves to achieve what's in the paintings."

—JOSH NADELBERG

Gulp's Overlook

🌀 *"I'm a bit more focused on the content than on the rendering style. I usually do a lot of drawings initially. I come from a drawing background. It's easier for me to visualize things via drawing and then fill in the blanks and fill in the materials and how everything works together—the lighting, the mood."*

—Johannes Figlhuber

WINTER TUNDRA

⟳ "The original game is made of very simple shapes. For Winter Tundra I worked on a really basic castle. I made a reference screenshot of the opening scene that shows the entire castle and then I did a design inspired by that. And then I did a color thumbnail. I also have color variations that I attached to the file."

—SERINA MO

⟳ "There are barriers and some challenges that I'm facing (with Winter Tundra), trying to figure out, What is the limitation of the concept? How bold can I be with my art?"

—SERINA MO

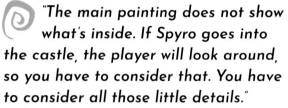

⟲ *"The main painting does not show what's inside. If Spyro goes into the castle, the player will look around, so you have to consider that. You have to consider all those little details."*

—SERINA MO

Mystic Marsh

"In Mystic Marsh, we had these buildings. They are egg-shaped, and I looked up references of African tribes and how they do pottery and necklaces and tried to take those elements—how they built this stuff—and make it look like the buildings are done by a similar process."

—Jakob Eirich

"For Mystic Marsh, I looked up the dragon tree, which has this big round trunk, and I tried to make a new kind of tree out of that, so this is the nature influence I took and made something more fun and fitting to the Spyro theme."

—Jakob Eirich

Cloud Temples

"Scale has to be taken into account. We had to be careful the player doesn't feel like a tiny fly next to . . . a bookshelf, for example."

—Didier Nguyen

Robotica Farms

"[Robotica Farms is about] a robot living in a nature farm, so I have to figure out how to combine those two, figure out how to make the design more Spyro-ish. Also, real-world images help for the mechanism in each building or all the props."

—SERINA MO

Canyon Speedway

![spiral icon] "John had such a good grasp of the shape language and the vibrant color palettes we were after. In Canyon Speedway he did a painting of the canyon rocks and gave them these great silhouettes. You're flying through the map so fast you probably don't notice."

—JOSH NADELBERG

Ripto's Arena

"[In Winter Tundra,] Ripto took over this castle. I also did the arena. He rides a dragon and attacks Spyro, and the lava comes up to the ground. For the original game, there is nothing on the ground. It's just a tiled floor. They fly, and [Ripto] throws a gem at Spyro, and the entire floor starts being covered by lava."

—SERINA MO

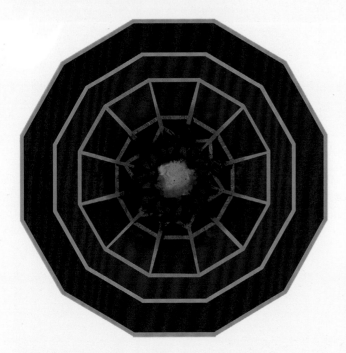

"So for me, I had to make this reasonable to make sense. So for the arena painting, I did a halo design that you can see through [to] the lava underneath, and then there's smoke coming out from it."

—SERINA MO

Dragon Shores

Dragon Shores is this park with a rollercoaster and games. In the original it didn't look like a park. It was more simple-looking and didn't have a lot of architecture in it. So I tried to make it a real fun amusement park."

—Jakob Eirich

"Dragon Shores was just this fun, chill, relaxing level at the end of the game after you beat the boss. In the original, it's a bit more simple. We took some liberties and changed up how the roller coaster looked."

—Johannes Figlhuber

Forgotten Realms
Spyro: Year of the Dragon

@ *"In Spyro 3, we were introduced to a whole new world, the Forgotten Realms. Once again, every level was an entirely new theme for us to reimagine. The amount of creativity that was poured into those was just staggering."*

—JOSH NADELBERG

"We had this funny pose of Spyro from the concept art that would show up in a lot of the environment paintings. The artists would plop him in there to help indicate scale. It kind of made me chuckle every time he'd show up. It's like a little surprise. You wouldn't notice him at first, and then all of a sudden, you'd see that silly raised eyebrow."

—JOSH NADELBERG

Molten Crater

Seashell Shore

"The size and scale of the levels really expanded in game 3 with the addition of the parts of the level that you'd play as the other heroes. The 3D artists had to extrapolate from the concept art to fill in a lot of blanks. I feel like we could have done twice as many paintings and still would have left a ton of stuff unexplored."

—JOSH NADELBERG

Mushroom Speedway

🌀 *"We tried to stick to the original mood because it was already very good, and we tried to embellish it, tried to make it more lifelike, more immersive."*

—Johannes Figlhuber

Sheila's Alp

Buzz's Dungeon

MIDDAY GARDENS

🌀 "As a concept artist, it's easy to get tied into repeating the same visual language, the same shape language, so sometimes when I'm exposed to new experiences, it allows me to think outside the box."

—RON KEE

🌀 "What I think of is what emotions I want to evoke with the colors I use. When I know it should be happy and fun, I know sunshine makes people happy, and nature and green and blue, these natural colors make people happy."

—JAKOB EIRICH

Icy Peak

Enchanted Towers

Spooky Swamp

Bamboo Terrace

Country Speedway

Sgt. Byrd's Base

EVENING LAKE

"*The glowing underwater portals in Evening Lake jumped off the page in the concept art. I couldn't wait to see how they looked in-game. I remember we spent quite a bit of time adjusting the underwater lighting in that level to try and capture the magic of the painting.*"

—Josh Nadelberg

Frozen Altars

Lost Fleet

Fireworks Factory

"Fireworks Factory was another fan favorite that we really wanted to make sing. The key painting set a great mood, and the environment artists kept coming back to that image as they were working." —Josh Nadelberg

Charmed Ridge

Honey Speedway

Bentley's Outpost

Scorch's Pit

"Scorch's Pit is set inside a giant beast. You can see the bones surrounding the arena and the sun setting in the distance. Arenas were fun to work on because they're so compact compared to the other levels. They're like little snacks compared to the rest of the game."

—Josh Nadelberg

MIDNIGHT MOUNTAIN

"We got pretty good at making crystals by the end of the project! Midnight Mountain had these majestic pink crystal mountains, and by the time we got to making it, I think we had hit our crystal stride."

—JOSH NADELBERG

"You have some playable areas, and you have to respect them, so you're thinking, 'Oh, that's going to restrain me,' but it forces you to find another way to design the environments— find new tricks to make the visuals compelling for the players."

—DIDIER NGUYEN

Starfish Reef

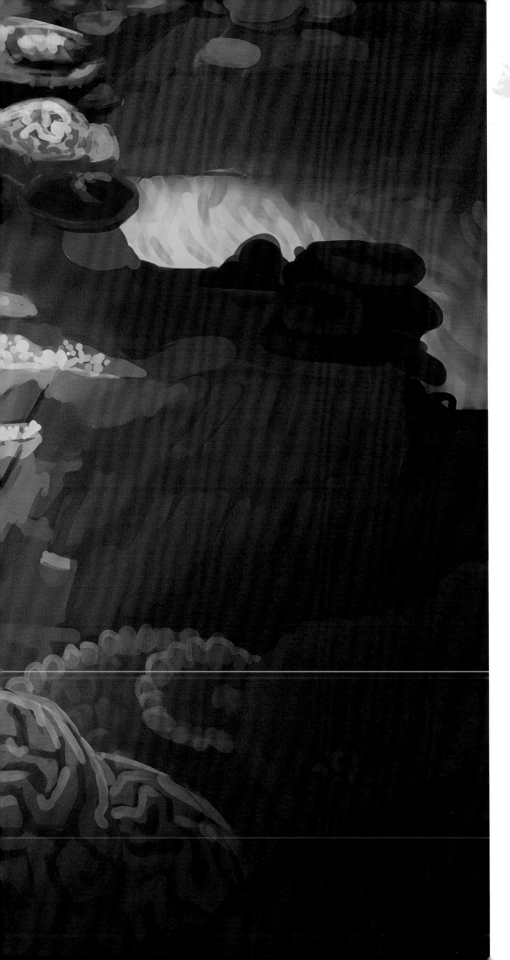

Crystal Island

Desert Ruins

Haunted Tomb

Dino Mines

"There's a great cut scene that takes place in Agent 9's Lab so we knew we needed to make sure it would hold up to a bit more scrutiny. We wanted to capture the lush, tropical quality from the concept art, and I remember spending some extra time to get that to feel good."

—Josh Nadelberg

Sorceress's Lair

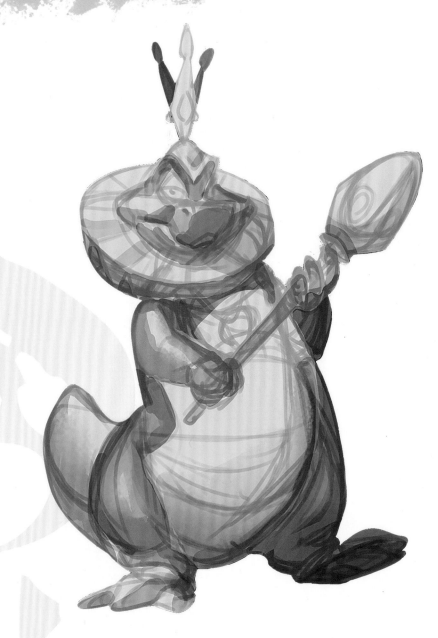

 "Working on the Spyro Reignited Trilogy was one of the most challenging things I've ever done. It took an army of amazing artists to make it happen. Looking back on it, I honestly can't belive how much work was put into the games. I'm exhausted all over again just thinking about it!"

—JOSH NADELBERG

CREDIT PAINTINGS

"Once we were done with all the content, we had a few of the concept artists work on some promotional illustrations. Devon did this sketch of Spyro with Gildas painting on the sidewalk, and I fell in love with it. That evolved into a whole series, which we ended up using as the credits rolled."

—JOSH NADELBERG

"The illustrations were really fun to do. Josh asked me to do one illustration, and then I proposed doing three, and then he's like, 'Can you make twelve?' So that was interesting. He liked the three enough that he wanted to make a calendar.

They were illustrations of Spyro interacting with each of his sort of 'Artisan dads.' The idea in my head was that he's not a very good artist yet, so all of his artist dads are training him to see if he likes what they do."

"It reminded me of old video game manual art. You don't really get manuals anymore, so it's nice to have that old-school watercolor look from the '90s. A lot of games had that line art with color underneath. That was one of the most fun projects I did for the whole game. They were printed out and put in the hallway at Toys For Bob."

—DEVON CADY-LEE

ACKNOWLEDGMENTS

"By the end, it was really hard to let the project go. I kept drawing dragons for a while. Occasionally, I'll continue to draw dragons and characters from the game just for fun."

—NICHOLAS KOLE

The incredible works collected in this volume were created by a team of artists from around the world who put their hearts and souls into the project. The fun we all had working together literally leaps from the pages of this book, and seeing it all presented like this reminds me of what a privilege it was to be a part of such a collaborative and supportive team. Thanks to all of you for your boundless creativity and inspiration!

While this collection is dedicated to the concept art, it took another gigantic army of brilliant 3D artists, animators, VFX artists, and game developers to translate all of these ideas into the visuals that you experience when you actually play Spyro Reignited Trilogy. A tremendous thank-you goes out to all of those folks at Toys For Bob and around the world who made the game a work of art as well!

Artist' Credits

Jeremy Anninos – pg. 28 (bottom middle), 29 (top left), 97 (colors), 104 (top), 107 (top), 116 (left)

Devon Cady-Lee – pg. 1, 15, 16 (middle), 17 (top left), 28-29, 49, 50 (top left), 51 (top left), 53, 55, 58-59, 60-61, 62-63, 67, 69, 72, 76, 78, 80-81, 82 (right), 83, 86, 88, 90 (right), 276-277, 278-279, 280-281, 282-283, 284-285, 286

Pedro Cardoso – pg. 5, 25 (top left), 40, 246-247, 250 (bottom), 251, 256 (left), 258-259, 261 (right), 264 (top), 268-269 (left, top right), 270 (top), 274-275, 287

Florian Coudray – pg. 178 (left), 180 (top left, bottom), 182 (top, middle), 183, 184, 185 (bottom right), 186-187, 188 -189 (top left, right), 210 (bottom), 211, 216-217 (right), 224-225 (top left, right), 235 (left, top right)

Isaac Davis – pg. 42, 43, 248, 252-253, 260-261 (left), 265, 272 (left)

Rob Duenas – pg. 6-7, 68, 82 (left), 91 (left), 92 (left), 100, 101 (left, top right), 132 (left), 137

Jakob Eirich – pg. 176-177, 202-203, 204-205 (left, middle), 212-213, 219, 234 (top), 242-243

Johannes Figlhuber – pg. 154-155, 159 (top left), 161 (top left, bottom), 165, 166, 198, 208 (tom middle, bottom)

Min Fu – pg. 218 (bottom), 228

I-Wei Huang – pg. 151 (top)

Ryan Jones – pg. 56, 64, 90 (left), 93, 123, 128, 131, 134 (left, top right, middle), 135

Ron Kee – pg. 158, 159 (bottom), 162-163, 164, 167, 196 (left), 222

Julie Kim – pg. 249, 23 (right)

Nicholas Kole – pg. 4, 8-9, 16 (top, bottom), (bottom, right), 19, 20, 21, 22, 23 (left), 24, 33, 38, 39, 46-47, 48, 52, 57, 65, 66, 71, 74 (w/ Murchie), 77, 79, 92 (bottom right), 95, 97, 105 (top), 118-119, 120 (left), 124, 125 (left), 130 (bottom), 132 (right), 133 (bottom left), 134 (bottom right), 136 (bottom left), 209 (top left), Cover, Endpapers

Simon Kopp – pg. 156-157, 159 (top right), 161 (top right), 173, 196-197 (right), 199, 200-201, 208 (top left, top right), 220-221

John Loren – pg. 98, 99 (bottom left), 101 (bottom right), 102-103, 104, 116 (right), 117, 209 (top right, bottom), 227, 237, 238-239

Mario Manzanares – pg. 160, 170-171, 205 (right), 206 (top left)

Serina Mo – pg. 206 (bottom), 223, 230-231, 232-233, 236, 240-241

Sarah Morris – pg. 193, 194 (bottom), 214-215, 229zzz

Mat Mossman – Pg. 41, 244-245, 250 (top), 254 (top), 255 (top), 256-257 (right), 262-263, 264 (bottom), 266-267, 269 (bottom), 272-273 (right)

Jeff Murchie – pg. 12 (left), 50 (bottom left, right), 51 (bottom left, right), 54, 70, 73, 74 (w/ Kole), 92 (top right)

Kristina Ness – pg. 216 (left)

Didier Nguyen – pg. 178-179, 180 (top right), 181, 182 (bottom), 185 (top right, middle right), 188 (bottom left), 210 (top), 224 (bottom left), 235 (bottom right)

Sylvain Sarrailh – pg. 190-191

Nicola Saviori – pg. 10, 12-13 (right), 26-27, 30-31, 34-35, 36-37, 45, 75, 84-85, 87, 89, 91 (right), 96, 99 (top left, right), 105 (bottom), 106, 107 (bottom right), 108-109, 110-111, 112, 114-115, 120 (right), 121, 122, 125 (right), 126-127, 129 (right), 133 (right), 136 (top, bottom right), 138-139, 288

Frederic Simon – pg. 2-3, 168-169, 172 (top left, top middle, bottom)

Geraud Soulie – pg. 172 (top right), 174-175, 206 (top right), 234 (bottom)

Billy Wimblett – pg. 190 (left), 192, 193 (top left), 194 (top), 195, 218 (top), 226

Oleg Yurkov – pg. 11, 32, 107 (bottom left), 113, 129 (left), 130 (top), 138 (top left)

Aletta Wenas – pg. 207

Ghostbot Inc. – pg. 140-141, 142-143, 144-145, 146-147, 148-149, 150, 151 (bottom), 254 (top), 255 (bottom), 270 (bottom), 271, 25 (left, bottom right)

COLOPHON

THE ART OF SPYRO
REIGNITED TRILOGY

ISBN: 9781789095647

Published by Titan Books
A division of Titan Publishing Group Ltd.
144 Southwark St.
London
SE1 0UP

FIRST EDITION: JULY 2020
3 5 7 9 10 8 6 4 2

DID YOU ENJOY THIS BOOK?

We love to hear from our readers. Please e-mail
us at: readerfeedback@titanemail.com or write to
Reader Feedback at the above address.

To receive advance information, news,
competitions, and exclusive offers online, please
sign up for the Titan newsletter on our website:
www.titanbooks.com

A CIP catalogue record for this title is available from
the British Library.

Printed and bound in China.